WRITE
THEMES
AND ESSAYS

JOHN McCALL
ASSOCIATE PROFESSOR OF ENGLISH
WISCONSIN STATE UNIVERSITY

MONARCH PRESS

CONTENTS

INTRODUCTION

TO THE STUDENT AND THE TEACHER

This book is intended for the first course in composition and can be used for any level of high school or college work where the emphasis is upon the writing of expository themes.

Much of the difficulty experienced by the beginning writer is that of organization: developing and presenting a clear and logical discussion. In fact, many teachers give a theme two grades: the one "above the line" is for grammar, spelling, punctuation, and so on; the one "below the line" is for organization (see A Typical Grade Sheet at the end of this book). The purpose of this book, then, is to help a student to improve his grade "below the line."

A note about the illustrative themes included: They are merely presented as examples of a particular form of development, not as themes of A, B, C, D, or F caliber, nor as themes of a new, imaginative, or memorable kind.

Only one of the themes is an example of literary analysis—see "An Analysis of 'A Description of a City Shower' " found in the DEFINITION-ANALYSIS section. The reason for not including more themes of this type is that literary analysis is a study in itself, beyond the scope and the purpose of this book. The beginning writer has far too many problems to cope with before he attempts to deal with the complexities of literary analysis.

TO THE STUDENT

"How do I go about writing a theme?" If you are asking yourself this question, this book tries to answer it as directly and as clearly as possible—without "talking down" to you or oversimplifying the process. Writing themes is not easy, for besides organizing your paper, you have many things to worry about:

grammar, spelling, punctuation, capitalization, details, effective wording, and so on. What you want, therefore, is a short, factual, to-the-point discussion of how to write a theme. Such a discussion is the promise of this book. A half-hour or so spent on any one section should enable you to write a theme which fulfills the requirements of whatever form of development you may select or have been assigned.

The first thing to remember is that the basic purpose of any communication is to convey ideas, thoughts, and feelings to someone else. Writing is one very important form of communication which you will use throughout your life. All writing (as well as speaking) can roughly be classified in one of four main categories: exposition, argument, description, and narrative. (These are sometimes referred to as the forms of discourse):

Exposition: This category includes most of what we write and read: textbooks, magazine articles, newspaper editorials, etc. Its purpose is to explain something: make an idea clear; convey a fact or a related series of facts; explain a process or a method, an organization or a system; etc. It includes either a presentation of factual material or an analysis of it, or both.

Argument: The central purpose of argumentative writing is to convince, to persuade the reader to adopt a certain idea, attitude, or course of action.

Description: The aim of description is to evoke the impression produced by some aspect of a person, place, scene, or the like. The writer tries to suggest in the reader's mind a picture similar to the picture in his own mind.

Narrative: The aim of narrative is to tell a story—to give meaning to an event or a series of related events. Fiction is known as plotted narrative. Non-fiction narrative writing may deal with events which are obviously significant (such as important events in history), or the writer may develop a significance in them by his particular treatment of the facts.

In high school and college the student usually has a chance

to develop his skill in all four categories. But it is highly probable that most of your papers in English composition classes will be expository—that is, exposition will be their central purpose. But since all four forms of writing can overlap, any composition you write will probably combine one or more of the methods described above. For example, your main purpose may be to explain how to do or how to build something (exposition), but you can add spice and human interest to the theme by adding a flashback (narration) which includes dialogue and action from your own experience. Examples of combinations of forms are given throughout this book in an effort to show how they may be combined to good advantage. In addition, specific examples of argumentative and descriptive themes have been included.

If your teacher has assigned a particular kind of theme, you should turn to the appropriate section in this book and read it through once to learn the broad principles. Then, follow the suggestions and the list of do's and don't's in writing your paper. Also check HOW TO BEGIN A THEME and HOW TO CONCLUDE A THEME at the end of this book. After you have completed your first draft, again go over the list to see if you have correctly followed the suggestions. Check each item. Of course, double-check your theme for every item on the PROOFREADING CHART, also at the end of the book. Once you have checked each and every item, then and only then should you write the final version to be turned in.

In many instances, your teacher will not specify a particular kind of development. Instead, the class is told to write on a particular topic, with the development left up to the student. This assignment need not be any more difficult than if the form of development were assigned. To help you decide, here are some specific suggestions about the most common forms of development.

DEDUCTIVE: Use this for any topic where you have two, three, or more items to discuss which deal with your main idea. This is by far the most common form of theme development and is used in perhaps 75 per cent of student themes.

INDUCTIVE: The opposite of deductive. Use it when you want to "save for the end" the main idea of your paper, when all the things you discuss lead to a conclusion, a moral, a lesson learned, a rule, and so on.

CLASSIC: It combines both deductive and inductive forms. Use it when you wish to repeat each of your main points three times—once in the introduction, once in the individual paragraphs, and once again in the conclusion. It is used frequently in arguments, sales talks, sermons, and the like.

CHRONOLOGICAL: An easy form of development. Use it when time plays a part from the beginning to the end of your theme —a trip, a vacation, your high school years, how to do something, and the like.

DESCRIPTIVE: Use when you know enough about a subject (or are interested enough in it to investigate it) to provide sufficient details to give the reader a clear picture or a dominant impression of the thing described.

HOW-TO; HOW IT IS DONE: Use the former if you are sufficiently expert on the topic. It implies that you have done it. Use the latter if you know enough about a topic to write a factual theme. It frequently means that you have to consult an authority or a printed discussion of the topic.

The following forms of development are used for specific purposes. In most cases, your teacher will give you the assignment.

ANALOGY: Use when you wish to explain something complicated by comparing it with something simple, or when you wish to compare two things which are ordinarily not considered to be alike.

ARGUMENT: Use this form with caution. Remember that "Nobody ever wins an argument" implies that your theme will also be on shaky ground, chiefly because all the facts and all the details have to be considered. If assigned to write an argumentative theme, state that you will present the facts to the best of your knowledge, and state that the reader has to make up his own mind.

BALANCED: Use when the discussion in the first half of the theme inevitably and logically leads to the second half. In other words, you have two main ideas in your theme, each of which takes up approximately half of the discussion. If you are not sure of this form of development, do not use it.

CAUSE AND EFFECT: Use when you wish to show the results (effect) of some event, idea, or action. You may develop the theme by showing how the causes led up to the effect, or you can state the effect(s) first.

CLASSIFICATION: Use when you wish to show how experts classify, or when you wish to show how you would classify items which share common features.

COMPARE AND CONTRAST: Use when you wish to show the similarities and differences between two or more things.

DEFINITION, ANALYSIS: Use when you wish to categorize, clarify, or explain confusing items, or when you wish to interpret or explain the "how" and the "why" of your personal opinion.

SUMMARY: Use only when specifically assigned by your teacher.

The other forms—FLASHBACK, IMITATIVE, and IMPLIED—are usually specifically assigned or are part of another form of development. The SPACE FILLER is included as an example of what not to do.

Remember that in beginning themes, your teacher is not so much concerned about literature as he is about literacy. What your teacher is looking for at first is a theme of perhaps three hundred words that states a thesis; that devotes two, three, or more paragraphs to developing that thesis; and that gives evidence of logical organization for proper communication of ideas.

How do we start? Let's take the most common form of development, that of the DEDUCTIVE, where you make a generalization (the thesis statement) in your opening sentences and discuss two, three, or more particulars in the following paragraphs. Let's assume that your teacher has given you an assignment to turn in a theme of two pages. Two pages may seem like a huge task, especially if you have never written that much before. How to fill two pages? Let's pretend that you own some guns: a pistol, a .22 caliber rifle, a .308 caliber rifle, a single-shot .410, and a double barreled .12 gauge. That's five guns—five paragraphs.

Let's stop a second. So you have five guns. What can you say about them? Whatever you can say about them becomes a generalization, a thesis sentence. You can make various generalizations: "My five guns have an interesting background." Then each succeeding paragraph will discuss the "interesting background" of each gun. Or, you can say "A hunter needs at least five guns to be equipped for all shooting situations." Again, you would discuss each gun in a separate paragraph, showing how each gun can be used for a particular purpose. Or, you can write about "How to aim a gun," "How to clean a gun," or "How the price of guns has gone up." If your theme becomes too long—remember a few minutes ago we were concerned about filling two pages—just discuss two or three guns.

So you don't own guns? Have you ever owned dogs? Two, three, or more dogs can be discussed just as well as two, three, or more guns. So can your brothers and sisters, the cars you have owned or would like to own, the hobbies you have, the teachers you have, the trips you have taken or would like to take, and so on. In short, any topic that can be broken down into two, three, four, or more parts can be a good theme topic.

To show how easy the process of writing is, let's pretend that you have not five, but three guns. The title is easy: My Three Guns. The thesis sentence will state what the three guns have in common. Let's say that this is your thesis: "My three guns are all I need to hunt with in this area." Let's put the sentence into an opening paragraph:

"At the present time, I own three guns: a Ruger Mark I target pistol, a Remington Model 600 carbine, and a Fox double barrel shotgun. My three guns are all I need to hunt with in this area. Let me explain."

You don't have to write any more than these three sentences. (Quotation marks are merely to show which of these paragraphs belongs to the theme and which belongs to this Introduction. The theme when written would not have quotation marks.) You mentioned the pistol first. So, you will make it the topic of your second paragraph. Describe it and say what kind of hunting you use it for:

"My first gun is a Ruger Mark I target pistol. It's a .22 caliber automatic which holds 9 long rifle cartridges. The barrel is 6⅞ inches, the pistol weighs 42 ounces, and the sights consist of a blade front and a click rear which is adjustable for windage and elevation. I use this gun not only for target practice, but also for shooting owls, crows, and vermin. Any small game which is legal to shoot at while sitting is good hunting. Many a Saturday I have spent in the local junk yard eliminating vermin, which are always plentiful and which afford me much practice."

The third paragraph talks about the next gun:

"My second gun is a Remington Model 600 carbine. It holds five .308 Winchester shells, weighs 5½ pounds, and is a fraction over 37 inches long. It's a beautiful gun and handles as though I were born with it in my hands. This carbine is perfect for hunting deer when the terrain is rough. Deer in this area are found only in thick brush, where a short rifle with plenty of shocking power and rapid firing is needed. The proof is in the field: Using this powerful little rifle, I have brought home a deer three seasons in a row."

And the fourth paragraph tells about the third gun:

"My third gun is a Fox double barreled .12 gauge shotgun. It is my pride and joy. It is chambered for 2¾ inch shells, is hammerless, has an automatic safety, and has the right barrel full choked and the left barrel modified choke. This gun is perfect for the many rabbits around my home town and is also

a wonderful gun to bring down the occasional duck which flies to the small pond near my home."

Now you need a concluding paragraph. You tie it in with your opening:

"In the near future I hope to buy a few more guns. But since the only game animals I have to hunt around my home town are the ones I have mentioned, the three guns I own are all I need to have a successful day's hunt."

You have written your theme. Put the five paragraphs together and they represent a competent, logical, organized presentation of a topic. The theme has a title which tells what you are going to discuss. It has a thesis which limits the area you are going to cover and also serves as part of the introductory paragraph. It has three paragraphs, each of which describes a gun and tells what hunting the gun is used for. (Note that the first sentence of paragraphs 2, 3, and 4 is the topic sentence of the paragraph.) And it has a concluding paragraph which "wraps up" the theme and makes it unified by repeating the thesis sentence.

We have mentioned the various things you can write about—hobbies, teachers, brothers and sisters, and so on. All you have to do is pick a topic that can be divided into parts. Here's a little chart that can be used to help you write your first theme:

My Three_____

(Thesis sentence in first paragraph) My three_____

_____

(Topic sentence of second paragraph) My first_____

_____

(Topic sentence of third paragraph) My second_____

_____

(Topic sentence of fourth paragraph) These are my three____

_____

(Fifth paragraph concludes the theme) These are my three__

_____ _____

With the blanks filled in, add a minimum of three or four sentences which discuss the words in the blanks in each paragraph, and you have a theme.

And now, turn to the section of this book which interests you or which you have been assigned and read it through. Following the suggestions and the list of do's and don't's read the sample themes and the analysis given for each theme. Then organize and write your theme. It's not so hard after all, is it?

CLASSIFICATION OF THEMES:

FORMS AND METHODS

ANALOGY

An analogy is defined as a relation or resemblance existing between two things; that is, one thing is like another thing in that they have similar characteristics, features, effects, etc. The more the two things share similar attributes the more they are like each other. Of course, the two things are also different in other respects. One is more advanced than the other, or it is more complicated than the other, or it is composed of the features of the other but also has additional features. In short, two things are discussed in terms of each other neither to show how much they are alike or to explain how the "complicated" is really the "simple" with advancements.

Thus, we can have analogies made between things at or on the same level: a photograph and a painting, a piano and an organ, rugby and football, a chicken and pheasant, a truck and a tractor, or stew and soup. Or, we can make an analogy between things on different levels: a child's balloon and a jet engine, a scout and a soldier, checkers and chess, a kite and a glider, or building a doghouse and building a home.

APPLICATION: Now study the suggestions and read the list of do's and don't's. Then read each theme, including the analysis given. As you read each theme, refer to the suggestions and the list to see how the theme has implemented them. Once you have a good idea of what to do, look at the suggested list of topics and decide what your topic will be. When you have written your first draft, recheck the suggestions to see if you have included everything.

SUGGESTIONS: The analogy is developed using one of the standard forms, usually DEDUCTIVE, INDUCTIVE, COM-

PARE AND CONTRAST, etc. Most themes based upon analogy are relatively short, chiefly because sustained analogy is either impossible, too strained, or because it becomes an exercise in trying to find similarities.

In a sustained analogy, you can either point out similarities in one paragraph, dissimilarities in another paragraph; or you can do both in one paragraph. See both forms of COMPARE AND CONTRAST. There is no formula conclusion in an analogy. See HOW TO CONCLUDE A THEME. As stated in the first paragraph above, most analogies are but part of another form of development.

DO'S AND DON'T'S:

1. Most analogies imply that the common, the simple, the known, is used to explain the uncommon, the complex, the unknown. Or, to put it another way, analogy is used when the complex is explained by breaking it down into simple parts with which the reader is familiar.

2. Make sure that the known is known to your reader. Generations of students have smiled at Samuel Johnson's definition of "network"—"anything reticulated or decussated"—as being more complex than the thing defined.

3. Be sure also to say why the complex is not like the simple. For example, a theme describing college to a group of high school students would point out both similarities and dissimilarities. See COMPARE AND CONTRAST.

4. Most of our everyday inferences are by analogy—from past experiences to future predictions. Most analogies are brief. Most analogies are found in other forms of writing: DEDUCTIVE, INDUCTIVE, COMPARE AND CONTRAST.

5. Literary analogies are called similies or metaphors and are used in describing, explaining, arguing, and the like.

6. Don't use figures of speech and let it go at that. Thus, to say that A is like B is not enough. You must explain why

A is like B, what they have in common and how they differ.

7. Don't use false analogy. That is, make sure the things in the analogy are similar, that the simple is a logical simplification of the complex or a logical simplification of part of the complex. If things are alike in one way, they may not be alike in others.

8. Don't try to explain the very difficult unless you are familiar with it.

9. Remember that no analogy is exact. The complex is only partially explained by the simple.

10. Check the PROOFREADING CHART.

SAMPLE THEME—ANALOGY—ITEMS ON SAME LEVEL:

How Knowledge and Atomic Energy are Alike

Knowledge and atomic energy are alike in that both can be used for either creative or destructive purposes. Both knowledge and atomic energy exist as latent or active.

Let us go back to the sources of knowledge and atomic energy. Knowledge begins as an idea, tiny and invisible in the human mind; atomic energy begins as an atom, invisible to the naked eye. Yet both the idea and the atom possess the potential for tremendous power. However, as long as they remain in the latent stage, neither the idea nor the atom can become constructive or destructive. Knowledge requires a reaction to ideas in the human mind before it can develop into the explosive power that is creative or destructive. As long as knowledge remains latent in stockpiles of books, it has no power of its own. So must the atom be activated by certain processes before it can become the explosive power that can be used for creative or destructive purposes.

Many constructive uses are now being found for atomic energy. One example of a good use is to generate electricity. The

Atomic Energy Commission is working on projects whereby atomic energy will be used to alleviate much of man's work, to provide the huge sources of power he will need, to be a servant to man in countless ways. But we all know the terrible destructive power of atomic energy which was demonstrated in Japan in 1945. And we all in some degree are living under the peril of sudden annihilation by even more advanced atomic bombs.

Similarly, knowledge has been activated and utilized by mankind. It has been put to countless constructive uses. It has produced inventions which have improved man's living conditions. It has been passed on from generation to generation in innumerable ways to keep mankind constantly advancing. In short, it is knowledge which has brought mankind so far. But we must confess that knowledge has also been used for destructive purposes. It has been used for warfare, for mass killings, for poisoning man's mind with evil ideologies, for arousing man's hatreds in a thousand ways.

So we may conclude that neither atomic energy nor knowledge has power within itself to become constructive or destructive. The way in which mankind uses each of them makes all the difference.

ANALYSIS: Note that the writer has wisely presented the basis of his analogy in the opening paragraph (see DEDUCTIVE). In two sentences, he tells the reader what areas of development the theme will present. The first sentence is also a good thesis sentence, because it summarizes the idea of both the first paragraph and the entire theme.

Because the two items under discussion are not really a simplification or an enlargement of each other, the author devotes paragraph two to a statement of his reasons for comparing what in reality are unrelated items. This is done because we commonly expect an analogy to have one item simpler than the second item so that the second item can be understood. This paragraph could well have been combined with the first paragraph.

Paragraph three discusses the good and bad sides of atomic

energy, and paragraph four does the same with knowledge. Since the opening paragraph promises such a discussion, these paragraphs are both logical and necessary. Note the excellent transitional word beginning paragraph four.

The conclusion is short, but note how effectively it repeats the opening thought. It also expands the thesis, inasmuch as the discussion in paragraphs two, three and four has lead the writer to such a conclusion. The final sentence is quite effective as a parting thought.

SAMPLE THEME—ANALOGY—ITEMS ON DIFFERENT LEVELS:

The Queen Bee

After I pledged a fraternity, I became aware of a type of girl on campus who is highly analogous to the queen bee in a hive. I think that the resemblance is remarkable.

The queen bee in a hive represents true royalty. Her instincts tell her that there can be only one leader in each hive. For this reason, she is quick to destroy or drive away any opposition. All the other bees live to serve her and to keep her well fed and protected The male bee is of no value except as a mate for the queen. He serves no other purpose, such as producing honey or fighting the enemies of the hive, as do the workers and the guard bees. Were it not for the queen, these drones would be killed or banished. The workers supply the queen with honey. The guards protect her with a barbed weapon called a stinger. In short, it appears as though thousands of bees exist solely to serve the queen bee.

Similarly, many sororities have a queen bee, a girl who represents true royalty. Any slight threat of opposition which might come from the "workers" or the "guards" meets with sudden and sure retaliation. Accordingly, they seldom show any signs of opposing her. Even a brief acquaintance with a sorority leads one to believe that all the other girls in the sorority exist to serve their "queen bee." She gets first choice of the males on campus who are leaders, wealthy athletes, or who have positions of power. These males become her escorts, her dates. Any other male not fitting into the above groups is automatically a "drone," and he is left for the inferior bees to fight over. The workers and the guard bees in the sorority serve the same functions as their counterparts in the hive. They maintain their queen's room, her clothing, her reputation—and frequently her scholastic standing. They are at her beck and call to serve as needed. On the whole, the girls seem to regard their queen with the same respect and awe that the bees regard their queen. Rather than a stinger, however, the girls have an equally pointed and deadly weapon—their tongues. A tongue, as any male knows, can paralyze or destroy an enemy as surely as a bee's stinger.

And so, the next time you are walking past a sorority house and hear a buzzing within, do not think that your ears are playing tricks. You, my friend, have just come across a real, honest-to-goodness, grown-up hive of human bees.

ANALYSIS: Like the previous theme using an analogy, this theme also begins with a short paragraph which effectively presents the author's topic. The second sentence promises the reader a "remarkable" resemblance, and the author does a good job in fully developing the resemblance.

There is a logical development in paragraphs two and three. Obviously, the queen bee and her role in the hive must first be discussed. Then, with the effective transition "similarly," the author switches to paragraph three to point out the "remarkable" analogy presented by the sorority "queen bee."

The conclusion is short, yet effective, in that it ends with the same tone—sarcastic, perhaps, but yet in keeping with the theme.

Note that this analogy is easier to make than that made in the previous theme. It also effectively discusses the complex (the sorority queen) in terms of the simple (the queen bee in the hive).

SUGGESTED TOPICS FOR ANALOGY THEMES:

1. High School and College

2. Student Government and State Government

3. A Theme and a Term Paper

4. Boy Scouts and Military Leaders

5. A Blueprint and a Map

6. A Sheet of Music and a Theme

7. A Gas-operated Rifle (needs research)

8. The New Mathematics (needs research)

9. How a Computer Works (needs research)

10. The Job Corps and the CCC Camps (needs research)

ARGUMENT

Handbooks (see the Bibliography at the end of this book) usually devote many pages to themes which present an argument, because argumentative themes are very difficult to write. The difficulty does not lie in the organization of the theme. Rather, it lies in having correct logic, in presenting suitable evidence, in making a valid generalization from the evidence presented, and of course, in presenting a better argument than one's opposition.

An argumentative theme is one which presents and develops reasons which lead to a generalization, or a conclusion, which in turn leads to an application. Thus, we present a number of instances of X causing Y to happen, and we then say that we should remove or modify X if we do not want Y to happen or if we want Y to happen in another way.

Because of the many difficulties involved, therefore, unless you have been specifically assigned to present an argument, or unless you have had special training in debating and logic, do one of two things: 1) avoid controversial topics, or 2) state you are merely presenting the two sides of an argument in order to allow the reader to decide for himself.

APPLICATION: Now study the suggestions and read the list of do's and don't's. Then read each theme, including the analysis given. As you read each theme, refer to the suggestions and the list to see how the theme has implemented them. Once you have a good idea of what to do, look at the suggested list of topics and decide what your topic will be. When you have written your first draft, recheck the suggestions to see if you have included everything.

SUGGESTIONS: Present the cause, reasons, and history of the controversy in the first paragraph. Tell the reader where you stand. Your conclusion will reaffirm your stand. If you wish to remain neutral, tell the reader that you are presenting both sides and that he is to make up his own mind.

In the second paragraph you can use one of two forms: Form 1: Discuss all of one side. It may take more than one paragraph. Form 2: Discuss point 1 of each side. If you have chosen sides, tell the reader why your side is the better one.

The following paragraph(s) is developed similarly: Form 1: Discuss all of the other side. Again, it may take more than one paragraph. Be sure you cover all the points made in the paragraph above. Form 2: Discuss point 2 of each side. If there are other sides, present them in succeeding paragraphs. If you use Form 2, use a separate paragraph for each subsequent point. As in the previous paragraphs, if you have chosen sides, say so.

In your conclusion, if you have chosen sides, reaffirm that your side is right because of the preceding evidence. If you remain neutral, tell the reader to decide.

DO'S AND DON'T'S:

1. Argumentative themes in which you take sides are extremely dangerous. Controversial subjects require much thought and research. Then, too, if you choose a harmless topic, you run the danger of writing a series of platitudes.

2. Use familiar subjects—campus politics, school activities, and the like.

3. Most argumentative themes imply that you take sides. If you write such a theme, tell the reader quickly which side you support. At the end of each paragraph, review why your side is right. In your conclusion, state that, for the reasons discussed, your side is right.

4. If you intend to remain neutral, quickly tell the reader that you are going to present both sides and let him make up his mind. See COMPARE AND CONTRAST.

5. No matter what approach you take, you must use up-to-date facts, figures, charts, quotations, authorities, and the like, for both sides. Do not use partial proof if it does not give an accurate account of your source. If you are quoting, be cautious in your use of ellipses, especially if the omitted material changes the meaning of your original source.

6. Define your terms. Be specific in what you mean by your terms.

7. Avoid generalizations by others or by yourself. Also avoid faulty logic, faulty analogies (see ANALOGY), inadequate presentation of evidence.

8. Remember that an argument must present strong evidence on all sides. If you choose a one-sided argument (for example, The Value of an Education), you are really not arguing. Such one-sided topics are best presented using other forms.

9. Avoid trying to disprove all that the opposition claims. Give credit where it is due. An argument that is willing to compromise on some issues is likely to be more fair and reasonable than one which stubbornly says that the opposition is completely wrong.

10. See also BALANCED, "The Proposed Honor System."

11. Check PROOFREADING CHART.

SAMPLE THEME—ARGUMENT (Form 1):

The "Bug" or the "Bomb"?

Having spent almost six years in the service and being a married man of twenty-five, I do not think that I am a typical freshman. I believe that I am more mature, more worldly-wise, and know the value of a dollar. My father-in-law, however, does not think that I know what I am doing, particularly when it comes to buying a car to replace the antique I am now driving. I want to buy a Volkswagen. He wants me to buy an American car. So our argument is for the "bug" or the "bomb."

Why do I want to buy a VW? First of all, it is my money. The VW I have priced costs about $1700.00, and that price includes everything I want on it. Once I have a VW, the cost of running it is very low. It gets thirty-two miles to the gallon, takes five pints of oil, and uses no antifreeze because it is air-cooled. The cost of insuring it is less than half of that of an American car. Repairs, if any are needed, are much cheaper, and the tires will last the life of the car if one rotates them and keeps them properly inflated. License plates are one-third the cost of a big car. These figures are facts, not fiction.

Then, too, the VW depreciates at a much lower rate than an American car. I have studied the prices in the papers for the past few months. A one-year-old VW depreciates about three hundred dollars, a two-year-old about four hundred, and a three-year-old about five hundred. In other words, I can drive a VW for three years and still get about two-thirds of my purchase price for it.

Furthermore, I want a car to drive to school, to church, to the grocery store. I do not plan to tour the United States with it. I want cheap, dependable transportation.

Now, there is nothing wrong with American cars. But in my situation, I have to look at the following facts. The car my father-in-law suggests that I buy will cost at least $2,500.00. It gets about twenty miles to the gallon, takes eight quarts of oil, and needs antifreeze. Insurance will cost well over one hundred dollars, repairs are expensive, license plates cost eighteen dollars. In short, the initial cost and the running expenses will be at least one-third more than with a VW.

How much does an American car depreciate? Too much, to my way of thinking. In the paragraphs above, I mentioned that a VW will depreciate about five hundred dollars in three years. An American car depreciates that much the moment it is driven out of the garage! And in three years, it will depreciate about 40 per cent, perhaps even more.

The American car, of course, does have advantages. It is a roomier, more comfortable car, especially for long trips. It is possibly a safer car. It is also a "status symbol" for Americans, but I can do without status for a while.

In short, there is a place for the VW and a place for the American car, and as long as I am a married college student, I insist that my place is in a VW, father-in-law notwithstanding.

ANALYSIS: Note the effective opening paragraph. The author quickly tells the reader what the controversy is—the thesis of the theme—and also gives some proof that he is an "authority" because he is mature.

Then, in paragraphs two, three, and four, the author amasses evidence supporting his side of the argument. He uses "then" and "furthermore" to show the reader that he is continuing one line of argument. Note that he provides ample evidence to back up his claim that he is presenting facts, not fiction. Also, the positive tone he uses gives his theme a valid, no-nonsense sound.

In paragraphs five, six, and seven, the author wisely concedes that the other side has some merit. But note how effectively he takes the same particulars used in arguing his side to demolish his opponent's position.

The conclusion is excellent. He concedes the merits of his opponent's side, but repeats that at present the facts are on his side.

SAMPLE THEME—ARGUMENT (Form 2):

Which Side Is the Student Council Taking?

Many of us students feel that the Student Council seems to be siding with the Administration, not with the students. In this paper, I intend to discuss three recent actions by the Council which have convinced me that it is not the voice of the student body.

First of all, the Council sided with the Administration in banning automobiles for freshman and sophomores. I cannot argue with a rule banning cars. It is obvious that there just isn't enough parking space on the campus to handle all the faculty and student cars. But it seems to me that if some exceptions are to be made, the Council should have as much say as the Administration. For instance, Fraternity Row just happens to have enough parking space, and so cars are permitted. Do I have to join a fraternity to have a car? I am twenty-one years old, but I am a freshman. As the rule now stands, a nineteen-year-old junior can have a car, but a freshman or sophomore, no matter what age, no matter what the conditions, cannot have a car. The Council should insist that special cases—and there are many—should be considered.

Next, the Council "recommended" that the proposal to increase activity fees to ten dollars a quarter is a good thing. With about ten thousand students on campus, at thirty dollars each for the school year, the figure comes to three hundred thousand dollars! For my thirty dollars, I will get to see four home football games, one out of three basketball games, and tennis, baseball, and track. I also get the school paper. If the Administration or the Council would show me how the three hundred thousand dollars is to be spent, I would be much happier. I know that education is expensive. But if the school needs the extra money, why not be honest about it and increase our tuition, not beat around the bush with increased activity fees?

And finally, our school paper should represent the students as much as it represents the Administration. The Council, however, meekly accepts whoever is recommended by the

Administration to be the "adviser" for the paper. "Censor" is the better word, for nothing of a controversial or critical nature is ever printed. I personally know of three or four letters to the paper which have never been printed. As I mentioned earlier, our student fees pay for the paper; should it not then be as much a voice of the students as it obviously is of the Administration?

I realize that the Administration and the Council should work together. I do feel, however, that if we are to have a Council, it should consider that it is the voice and the safeguard of the students. If it neglects us, who will speak for us?

ANALYSIS: This theme is not so effective as the previous theme. The opening paragraph presents the thesis and says that there are three reasons for making such a statement. As such, it is a good paragraph. Then, in paragraphs two, three, and four, each of the reasons is discussed. Again, the organization is good.

But the first reason is more of a whine that the author is a "special case" than it is part of the proof. The second reason also continues the petulant tone and indulges in name calling, hinting strongly that the college is deviously going about increasing costs. And in the fourth paragraph, the author has but one claim—"three or four letters" is hardly sufficient proof.

In short, what the author has presented is not a factual, solid argument, but three charges that quickly amount to a personal lament. Note that the final paragraph changes tone, that it is subdued, not nearly so caustic as the three paragraphs which lead to it. If the author's "facts" made his tone so positive in paragraphs two, three, and four, he should have ended as strongly. In presenting his case, what the author has given us is emotion, not facts.

SUGGESTED TOPICS FOR ARGUMENT THEMES:

1. Should a Student "Snitch" on Cheaters?

2. Commuting *vs.* Living at College

3. Should Students Have Cars?

4. University *vs* Private Housing

5. Fraternity Life *vs.* Independent Life

6. Education *vs.* Experience

7. The Military Draft

8. Vote Dry, Drink Wet

9. Athletic Scholarships

10. Scholarship *vs.* Activities

BALANCED

A balanced theme is one in which the first half of the presentation logically and inevitably leads to the second half. In short, it is a theme of two parts: the facts, details, etc., of the first half result in the effect or the conclusion which the second half discusses. Thus, while a deductive development has the generalization early in the theme, and the inductive development has the generalization late in the theme, the balanced development has its generalization, its key statement, its thesis, in the middle of the theme, and the remainder of the theme discusses it.

Be sure of one thing when using the balanced form: ask yourself if either half can stand alone. If so, your theme is incorrect. This faulty development is called "broken-backed." The one sure way to avoid it is to have your first half cause the second half: a week's rain brought on this result, the following violations brought on this rule, if that occurs then this will happen, and so on. If you are still not sure of yourself, choose some other form of development.

APPLICATION: Now study the suggestions and read the list of do's and don't's. Then read each theme, including the analysis given. As you read each theme, refer to the suggestions and the list to see how the theme has implemented them. Once you have a good idea of what to do, look at the suggested list of topics and decide what your topic will be. When you have written your first draft, recheck the suggestions to see if you have included everything.

SUGGESTIONS: If writing a "come on" theme, you will have two or three paragraphs before generalizing. If writing a "switch" theme, you will discuss all of A before discussing all of B. See ARGUMENT, Form 1, and COMPARE AND CONTRAST, Form 1. Your "come on" may well continue for another paragraph or two, depending upon the amount of detail you present before reaching your topic or thesis sentence.

The generalization or thesis is placed in mid-theme. If contrasting, use words like *but, on the other hand.* If comparing, use words like *similarly, also, in a like manner.* See COMPARE AND CONTRAST. After the reason for your "come on" has been stated, develop the generalization further in preparation for the conclusion. If you have "switched," you devote the remainder of your theme to whatever you switched to. The conclusion for either the "come on" or the "switch" could restate your generalization, or it could conclude by commenting on both A and B.

DO'S AND DON'T'S:

1. Unless you are sure of yourself, do not wait until mid-theme to state your thesis or generalization (the "come on" approach). It is safer to use the DEDUCTIVE approach, especially if you will do nothing but ramble until you state your thesis.

2. The balanced form using the "switch" approach is similar to COMPARE AND CONTRAST, Form 1, or to the ARGUMENT, Form 1. This balanced form implies that the two things under discussion are dependent upon one another, or are opposed, alternate choices, and the like.

3. If you are contrasting, use such words to introduce the other point as "But," "On the other hand," "If we look at the other side," and so on.

4. If you use the "switch" approach (where the topics are dependent upon each other), use such words as "Similarly," "In like manner," "Also," and so on.

5. Be careful that you do not have a "broken-back" theme. That is, if you are using the "switch" technique, be sure that the topics are mutually dependent. Do not write a theme, for instance, in which the first half talks about your home town, and the second half about your pets. The "switch" technique is best used for two sides of an argument, for comparing and contrasting, and the like.

6. For another type of balanced form, see CLASSIC

7. Check the PROOFREADING CHART.

SAMPLE THEME—BALANCED—"COME ON":

The New Rules for Girls

It is spring again on campus, and the inevitable spring customs are in full bloom, among which is the revival of open love-making on campus. Of course, during the entire school year, one may see hand-holders and polite goodnight kisses near any girls' dormitory, but in the spring more obvious signs of affection are in evidence.

There are other reasons for more obvious love-making than the traditional explanation—that it is spring. The prospects of a long summer are before the lovers, and each will go his or her way until next September. The long three months seem like an eternity to people who must part. There is much sentimentality involved, too, because many students, despite what they may say, become emotional at the thought of another school year coming to a close. For instance, I for one hate the thought of final examinations and of term papers which are due, but once these are out of the way, that inevitable feeling of sadness overcomes me at the thought of another year gone forever. I imagine that emotions such as these are the cause of the many manifestations of open love-making seen on the campus.

And so, the good Dean of Women has come up with a new ruling that we students regard as remarkable for its short-sightedness: There is to be no parking on campus at night. What she means by this rule is that no girl is allowed to sit in a car anywhere on campus during the evening and night hours.

What does this rule lead to? It is clear that none of us girls are going to violate the rule, if for no other reason than the fact that the campus police are quite obviously present near the girls' dormitories and the parking lots. What is going to happen, of course, is exactly what the huge sign hanging from the flagpole on campus says will happen: the authorities at school are forcing young couples to flee to the "back roads and bushes." I understand that the Dean of Women became very irritated by the sign, but most of us students feel that she deserves all she is getting. She was probably justified in cautioning the girls about their behavior, but we feel that in making such a ridiculous rule, she will bring on results much worse than the evil she tried to rectify. Luckily, there are just a few weeks left in the quarter; I imagine that by fall the rule will be conveniently forgotten.

ANALYSIS: The opening paragraphs are good in that they arouse interest and also effectively present the author's point of view for the reasons behind open love-making on campus. What resulted from the practice is effectively included in the short third paragraph, which also serves to "switch" to the other half of the theme. As such, paragraph three is an excellent transition.

The concluding paragraph presents what the author feels will be the result of the rule and predicts that the rule will be forgotten during the summer vacation. The theme is thus a good illustration of a balanced approach, where one topic leads to another smoothly and logically.

SAMPLE THEME—BALANCED—"SWITCH":

The Proposed Honor System

The Student Council has been spending a great deal of time

debating the merits of installing an honor system on campus. All sorts of suggestions are being made about what an honor system should be, but basically it seems to be concerned with the book store's acquiring "little blue books" which the students will use when writing examinations. On the cover of the booklet will be a statement to the effect that the student signs his name in good faith that he has not cheated on the examination. Of course, there is a place for the student's name on the booklet immediately below the pledge. The student could sign his name somewhere else on the cover if he so wishes, and the teacher could then interpret it in any way he wished.

Another possibility suggested for the honor system is that the teacher will not have to be in the room when examinations are taken. The students will thus feel that they are not being "policed." Still another suggestion is that all papers written outside of class will also have a folder which will have the pledge printed on it. Thus there will be no cheating on term papers.

On the surface, such an honor system sounds good. The school paper and the local paper will feature the installation of the honor system, and various teachers, preachers, and administrators will deliver long-winded speeches about today's youth being mature, honest, or what have you.

But, I have some serious objections to the honor system. My high school had the system, and for four years, I saw what really happens.

First of all, there will be cheaters no matter what pledge is signed. A student in danger of failing a course has too great a temptation placed upon him. Facing the prospect of failing, of being put on probation, or of being thrown out of school, many students will grasp at any straw. I have seen it happen many times.

Secondly, I want the teacher to be in the room when I am taking an examination. I have yet to see a perfect examination. Some students will always have questions about wording, about what is meant, about this or that or the other. Only the person who made out the examination can answer such questions.

And last, I do not feel as though I am being policed, nor do any of the students with whom I have talked feel as though they are cheaters because the teacher remains in the room. I understand that the school has a system whereby young faculty can expect a senior member of the department to visit the classroom for observation purposes. If the Administration feels as though its young faculty could use some on-the-spot checking, why should we students feel that we can do without it?

Thus I maintain that while the honor system sounds good, especially to the public relations department and to the do-gooders, in practice it is but a shallow system that is violated just as often as when there was no honor system at all.

ANALYSIS: We have a good balanced approach in this theme. Paragraphs one, two, and three present what the honor system will be like and how it will be regarded. Then, as illustrated in the other balanced theme in this section, we have an effective short transitional paragraph—"But, I have some serious objections. . . ." In a balanced theme, such a transitional technique is mandatory.

The second half of the theme is also well organized. Note the use of "First of all," "Secondly," and "And last" to introduce the three paragraphs. The three paragraphs also present good reasons for the author to feel as he does. The concluding paragraph is thus appropriate because it is justified by the discussion which leads to it.

SUGGESTED TOPICS FOR BALANCED THEMES:

1. Required Assemblies

2. Cars as Necessities or as Status Symbols

3. Rules for Girls

4. College Education for All?

5. The Right to Own a Gun

6. ROTC—Fact and Fable

7. Our Library, Friend or Foe?

8. It's a Friendlier Place. But . . .

9. Bigger and Better for What?

10. Is This What We Were Promised?

CAUSE AND EFFECT

Cause and effect themes are developed using one of the other forms presented in this book, usually inductive, deductive, or balanced. In a sense, you are often arguing in a cause and effect presentation: this event or action has brought on or will bring about a certain effect (or effects). Be careful—you must thoroughly establish that the things you discuss logically and inevitably result in the effect you claim has happened or will happen.

You are familiar enough with the scientific method to know that a few experiments are not sufficient to make very solid claims. Therefore, avoid choosing controversial or broad abstract topics for cause and effect development, for instance, themes concerned with government, politics, religion, education, and the like. A short theme does not allow enough space to establish a convincing cause-and-effect analysis. Rather than try to prove something controversial to the reader which is original with yourself, choose instead to present that which others have discovered or proved, or that which happened to you—buying old cars costs you money, not organizing your studying caused you to get behind, and the like.

APPLICATION: Now study the suggestions and read the list of do's and don't's. Then read each theme, including the analysis given. As you read each theme, refer to the suggestions and the list to see how the theme has implemented them. Once you have a good idea of what to do, look at the suggested list of topics and decide what your topic will be. When you have written your first draft, recheck the suggestions to see if you have included everything.

SUGGESTIONS: You can begin your theme by discussing the

effect (see DEDUCTIVE), or by listing the causes and saving the effect for your conclusion (see INDUCTIVE). Your following paragraphs will discuss the causes in one of several possible orders: chronological, increasing importance, causal relationship. The order depends upon your topic and your approach to it.

Begin the second paragraph with Cause 1. Use any logical order in each paragraph. You could give the effect of the cause, or you could save the effect for your conclusion. Cause 2, Cause 3, etc., can be handled in the same way, usually in separate paragraphs. Again, you could give the effect of these causes, or you could save the effect for your conclusion. Exceptions can be handled as they occur, or you could devote separate paragraphs to them.

Your conclusion can discuss your opinion, your qualifying summation, or it could show the effect the above causes lead to.

DO'S AND DON'T'S:

1. Cause and effect is essentially a "particular to general" approach (see INDUCTIVE). However, the DEDUCTIVE form (the effect is mentioned and then the causes are discussed) is frequently the form used in written reports.

2. Make sure that you have sufficient evidence. If you cannot make definite statements, then qualify your remarks with words like *usually, possibly, it seems, apparently, probably,* and the like.

3. Do not ignore second and third causes. For instance, a successful fisherman who gets results ("effects") is successful for many causes, not just because he's using a brand name reel.

4. Beware of the fallacy of appealing to great names or to other authorities as a substitute for proving your case on its own merits.

5. Be sure that your facts, figures, authorities, etc., are valid.

6. A cause-and-effect theme is difficult to write. You will note that most discussions of the type are written by specialists. Unless you are writing about a personal experience, you will have to rely upon research to back your statements. You will frequently find topics and authorities mentioned in such courses as history, sociology, psychology, education, and so forth.

7. Don't assume that a cause which precedes an effect is a true cause; or that two things occurring simultaneously are related. The essence of cause and effect is repeated observation—the scientific method.

8. Don't rely on generalizations. A sentence like "Everybody knows that an education is necessary" may sound good, but it is not proof. If you must generalize, use the words found in the "Qualifiers" part of DEFINITIONS.

9. Don't ignore the exceptions. That is, if the causes lead to a certain effect nine out of ten times, you must not ignore the tenth time.

10. Check the PROOFREADING CHART.

SAMPLE THEME—CAUSE AND EFFECT—INDUCTIVE:

The Bad New Days

My father grew up in the southern part of the state, and I grew up in the southern part of the state. From my father, I have inherited a love for the outdoors, particularly a love for fishing. All fishermen have a bit of exaggeration in their character, it is true, but when my father talks about what fishing used to be like in the "good old days," I am inclined to believe him. I have to take his words on trust because what we have today certainly bears no resemblance to what he describes. These are truly the "bad new days."

The Big River, Father tells me, once swarmed with small-mouth bass. The water ran clear, there were deep pools of shaded water, and any fisherman could go home with a limit. Today, inadequate laws which allow small communities to dump their raw sewage into the river have turned the Big River into an open sewer. The few fishermen who visit its banks are seeking only carp or catfish.

The local reservoir was once a two-hundred acre hotspot, or so Father says. Today, gizzard shad and catfish have driven out all the game fish. At one time, no live bait could be used, but sometime in the past, some idiot dumped his illegal live bait into the reservoir, and inevitably the trash fish took over.

Green Lake is still a beautiful lake. It looks like a "fish" lake. It still has a reputation, largely undeserved, of being a lake for big bass. There are probably some eight- or nine-pounders in the lake. But look at its shores. Dozens of commercial and private camps, black-topped roads, rules, regulations, swimming beaches—it's like fishing in a fountain in the city square. A fisherman is hardly ever out of sight of campers, picnickers, speedboaters, and onlookers.

And Big Indian Lake can now be described as a muddy bowl. It, too, was once a fisherman's paradise. But look at it today. Black-topped roads swarming with speeders, the shores marred by beer cans and picnic litter. I imagine that a beach in a city looks pretty much like this on a Sunday afternoon. Also, sedimentation has set in. The lake is one vast shallow saucer of brown water. And when the hundreds of speedboats and water skiers finish their weekend desecrations, it takes three or four days for the water to clear.

The effect of all this is quite obvious. Fishing has become something the old-timers talk about and something the younger generation approach in a desultory manner. Whatever may have been gained by others, the fisherman has lost out. It is a common thing for true fishermen in our section to get in their cars and drive hundreds of miles to fish. Imagine, to find fishing we have to leave an area that boasts three or four lakes! And unless other areas wake up, they will eventually find that their local fishing waters have also been destroyed.

ANALYSIS: In this interesting introduction the author presents the thesis that these are "bad new days" and suggests that the facts will support his claim. Then, in paragraphs two, three, four, and five, he presents his evidence. In four well-written paragraphs, he gives the causes of the destruction of four fishing spots. Note that each of the paragraphs also has an effect. Then, in the final paragraph, the overall effect is presented: because fishing is poor, people have either quit fishing or must travel many miles to find good fishing.

The final sentence is valid: the causes and effects justify the statement. Note that this is an inductive conclusion. The last sentence could be placed at the beginning of the theme, making it a DEDUCTIVE development, or it could be used in both the introduction and the conclusion, making it a CLASSIC development.

SAMPLE THEME—CAUSE AND EFFECT—DEDUCTIVE:

The Sleeping Giant Is Restless

There is a rising tide of unrest in Asia which is causing that vast continent to become one of the smoldering trouble spots of the world. It seems to me that several factors account for this mass restlessness. Some of the causes are apparent, and in this paper I shall discuss four of them.

Most of us would agree that the main cause for Asia's unrest is her over-population. This over-population is the result of complex causes, some of which are scientific and medical: the death rate has been reduced, but little has been done to curtail the birth rate. The overcrowded and unfavorable living conditions brought on by this rapid population increase have produced a restlessness that will not be easily remedied.

The second cause for Asia's unrest is her diminishing food supply. In our sociology classes we learned that with a population of more than ten people per square mile, Asia's arable land will not produce enough food. Consequently, a large percentage of the people never get enough to eat. When large numbers of people go to bed hungry, deep unrest and dissatisfaction are inevitable.

A third reason for Asia's unrest is her contact with the West. To the Asians, the West represents a much higher standard of living than Asia can provide. This contact has caused them to want some of the material possessions that the West enjoys. The Asians are no longer satisfied with our surplus food and used clothing. They want a better way of life. It is understandable how this envy, coupled with unfulfilled desires, can cause such unrest as Asia is experiencing.

The fourth reason for this restlessness is Asia's mass illiteracy. The Asians are now beginning to realize that to have the standard of living they crave, their illiteracy must be reduced. So they are crying for education. But, here again, they are frustrated in this desire—another vacuum of need with little chance of fulfillment.

And so for the reasons I have mentioned—over population, not enough food, envy of the West, and illiteracy—Asia is restless. Each of these problems is monumental, each is being attacked, and each will cause restlessness for many years to come. Neither Asia nor the West, however, can throw up its hands in despair. The problems must be faced and dealt with, or they will most certainly lead to even greater ones.

ANALYSIS: In this DEDUCTIVE development, the author gives the effect first and then tells the reader he will discuss four causes of the effect. As such, it is a good opening paragraph. He could have reversed his development by saying the effect for his conclusion, organizing the theme with an INDUCTIVE development. Then, in paragraphs two, three, four, and five, each of the causes is discussed. Note that paragraphing "takes care of itself" when the author says that he will discuss each cause in turn.

The conclusion effectively repeats the four causes and the effect. The author wisely predicts that the problems are real and that they must be dealt with. Note that while cause-and-effect themes frequently are argumentative, this theme presents factual concretes (illiteracy, lack of food, etc.) are considered self-evident. four logical causes without establishing a chain of proof. The

SUGGESTED TOPICS FOR CAUSE-AND-EFFECT THEMES:

  1. The Causes of Failure

2. Why Change Majors?

3. A Winning Season

4. Our Dropout Problem

5. TV Rating Systems

6. The Booming College Population

7. Downfall of a Tyrant

8. Why........Was Defeated

9. Why We Need More Student Government

10. Are the Teens Dominating America?

CHRONOLOGICAL

Like the DEDUCTIVE form, a chronological theme is frequently assigned by the teacher or decided upon by the student because of the ease of development: you begin at the beginning and discuss each event or detail as it actually occurs in time.

But there are dangers in a chronological development. The first is that it is frequently boring to the reader. Do not, then, try to cover each and every detail of a week's trip to New York. Rather, compress the uneventful details, major passages of time when nothing happened, and the like, into a sentence or two. This leaves you free to select the three or four high spots of the trip and discuss them in detail. Your theme will be much more interesting if you follow this suggestion.

Secondly, paragraphing sometimes is difficult. Unless your chronology can be broken down into three or four events which can serve as topic sentences, you will have to use your judgment when to paragraph.

And thirdly, select something which really is of interest to you, something that really is a high spot of your life. If you are "bored with it all," your tone will be flat, stale, uninteresting.

In short, unless you are vitally enthusiastic, your theme will reflect your lack of enthusiasm.

APPLICATION: Now study the suggestions and read the list of do's and don't's. Then read each theme, including the analysis given. As you read each theme, refer to the suggestions and the list to see how the theme has 'implemented them. Once you have a good idea of what to do, look at the suggested list of topics and decide what your topic will be. When you have written your first draft, recheck the suggestions to see if you have included everything.

SUGGESTIONS: Your introduction could begin immediately with the sequence of events, or it could consist of prefatory remarks which tell the reader what you are about to discuss. You might also begin by using FLASHBACK form.

Paragraphs in a chronological paper could use the usual topic sentence, or they could be built upon a period of time, or a related series of activities. Frequently a short transition can be inserted to denote the passage of time. If there is a big gap in time, you could use a short transitional paragraph.

The chronology could end in the fourth, fifth, or sixth paragraph, with the final paragraph reserved for concluding remarks. Or your chronology could end in the final paragraph, with perhaps one or two sentences serving as a conclusion. Avoid trite endings like "Tired, but happy . . ."

DO'S AND DON'T'S:

1. A chronological development is perhaps the easiest form of theme construction. Remember, however, that you do not have to tell everything, to account for every minute, hour, day, week, month, or year, in a chronological theme. For instance, if you are to tell about a fishing trip, the dreary list of everything that happened from the time you got up in the morning until you returned home late that evening can frequently be reduced. The rule of thumb is to begin as close to the conclusion as possible.

2. Note that using the FLASHBACK form is a frequent and acceptable variation of the strict chronological approach, especially when action is involved.

3. In HOW-TO, HOW IT IS DONE themes, strict adherence to chronology is required.

4. Especially in short papers, you can bridge the gap by using transitions. If what you did next is of little or no importance to your theme, it is acceptable to use transitions like the following: "The following day," "The next week," "Three hours later," "When we arrived," "After spending a long week," and so on.

5. Avoid saying such things as: "I forgot to mention in the beginning that . . .," "Perhaps I should have mentioned earlier that . . .," and so on. Instead, go back to where you meant to say it and say it.

6. Do not reverse chronology (flashbacks are acceptable) for a paper discussing, say, your high school days.

7. Do not use an endless parade of similar expressions. Do not keep saying words like *then, and then, next, the next thing,* and so on. Especially avoid using the same word over and over.

8. Most chronological themes are too long, mainly because the author includes too much trivial detail. As in other forms of theme development, you should make a preliminary plan of your approach, striving to cover only the important, interesting things.

9. Check the PROOFREADING CHART.

SAMPLE THEME—CHRONOLOGICAL:

Journey to Nowhere

A week before Thanksgiving vacation, three of the fellows in my dormitory and I decided to go to Florida rather than go home for Thanksgiving. Accordingly, after two of them finished their eleven o'clock classes on the Wednesday before Thanksgiving, we piled into a car and headed south. Our preparations included taking beer can openers, sweat shirts with the college name on them, and a grand total of about forty dollars. We should have prepared a little more.

The car was perhaps a bit too old, eight years to be exact. It does not take a great deal of insight to predict what happened to us. We managed to get as far as Cairo, Illinois, before our first mishap, a blowout on the right rear wheel. The spare we put on didn't look much better than the tire we had to discard, but it did hold air. We wisely decided not to go over fifty-five miles an hour for the remainder of the trip, which meant that we had at least twenty-four hours of driving yet ahead of us.

From then on, we planned more carefully, or so we thought. One of the fellows from Tennessee remembered that there was a gas war going on in western Tennessee, and so we decided not to buy gas until we could save three or four cents on each gallon. As we passed through Jackson, Tennessee, we kept watching for the gas prices as we passed each service station. Again, you have guessed what happened. It took almost two hours for one of us to hitchhike to the next town, to buy a gallon of gas, and hitchhike back.

Good things and bad things, so the saying goes, happen in threes, so as we drove along farther south we kept waiting for the third bad thing. But nothing happened, at least for the next three or four hours. We planned to drive straight on through, of course, and so along about ten o'clock at night, we were sailing smoothly along somewhere in the wilds of Mississippi. I say "wilds" because when our generator finally went out, we were in absolute darkness. There was not a light in any direction, a combination of mist and fog began to shroud us, and traffic was at a minimum. As we sat there in the dark, we added to the store of curse words that enrich our language. It was around two or three o'clock in the morning before a state trooper came along—the first car to come along, by the way—and towed us into town. We slept in the car until morning. Since it was Thanksgiving, it took a great deal of persuasion to finally get a local mechanic to open his shop for us.

While waiting for the car to be repaired, we finally took stock of our situation. Our money was rapidly disappearing, we weren't even halfway to our destination, and we were far behind schedule. When the car was repaired, I got behind the wheel, made a north turn, and headed back for the campus. No one protested. We ate our Thanksgiving hamburgers at a drive-in somewhere in Kentucky. I wonder if we would have had a better time in Daytona Beach?

ANALYSIS: In five paragraphs, the author has written an interesting theme, with the chronology taking care of itself by the very nature of the theme. The introduction sets up the details of the chronology. Note that it is an interesting opening, one which attracts the reader's attention. The concluding line of paragraph one is a good foreshadowing of the events the author is to narrate.

Each succeeding paragraph handles a major episode of the trip—a blowout, running out of gas, and the failure of the generator. The final paragraph is good. While it is not a surprise ending (the introduction gives a clue that the events will be unfortunate), it continues the tone of the theme, and it ends on a light touch.

SAMPLE THEME—CHRONOLOGICAL:

Home Town: U.S.A.

My sociology teacher remarked in class the other day that one person out of ten will move this year, and that accordingly, the United States is rapidly becoming a nation of rootless people. I know what he means, for I have lived in so many towns and have gone to so many schools that they are all beginning to become a blur in my mind. I would have to say that I am almost as rootless as a hobo. My "home town" is where I happen to be at the moment.

This rootlessness is caused by my father's work: he's a "trouble shooter" for a management consultant firm with headquarters in Chicago. He works chiefly with big corporations, state highway departments, and the like, so that he frequently spends a year or two on one job. Since I am an only child and since we rent homes, Mother and I have moved frequently with Father.

I grew up in Chicago and attended my first six years of school there. What childhood friends I have would be in Chicago, but since we have lived in three different areas, it becomes three different towns in my mind. I can remember only a few of the names of my childhood friends. I can't remember the name of one of the schools I attended.

For the next two years we lived in Peoria, Illinois. During that time I finished seventh grade in one school, and then I went for one year to junior high school. I made one friend that year, with whom I still correspond.

The following year found us in Springfield, Illinois. My memory of that year is centered chiefly around the basketball team which went to the state tournament. There are two students here at college who were in my class, but I don't recall them, and they don't remember me.

My tenth year of school was spent in Milwaukee, Wisconsin. Again, the school and the town are a blur in my mind. I remember a few more teachers and a few more of the students' names, but Milwaukee rapidly became only a name. I'm sure that I would feel like a stranger there if I should return to my old neighborhood.

My last two years were spent back in Chicago, but it was a suburb on the far south side, miles away from the neighborhoods in which I lived as a child. For my school records, that's my present "home town," but since my father is now in Toledo, Ohio, my mother will probably join him.

I intend to stay here in college until I graduate. I already have more friends here at college than I have had in all the time before coming to college. I am growing tired of moving and want to take roots for a while. Who knows, perhaps in the future I will look back to this college town as being my "home town."

ANALYSIS: This theme has a good opening paragraph. It gives the background of the exposition and it also arouses interest in what is to follow. Note that the introduction continues in the second paragraph. This paragraph could be included in the first paragraph.

Paragraphs three, four, five, six and seven then logically develop in chronological order. The paragraphs are short; yet each one gives us just enough details to tie in with what the author says in his introduction. Note that this theme is not so interesting as the previous theme. This is chiefly because the author is forced to say the same thing five times—the reader thus expects what is to follow. Note, however, that the author has a better method for moving forward than simply using "then" over and over. Study the opening sentences for his intelligent use of the word "year."

SUGGESTED TOPICS FOR CHRONOLOGICAL THEMES:

1. A Day I'll Never Forget

2. A Case of Mob Action

3. Man—Nature's Worst Enemy

4. A Sportsman's Paradise

5. Experience Pays Dividends

6. A Loser Becomes a Winner

7. How I Won the Prize

8. There's More to Cooking than Recipes

9. I Learned the Hard Way

10. Let's Save Our Resources

CLASSIC

The classic form of development is usually best reserved for speeches or written accounts that are long: the repetition in such cases serves to remind the listener or reader of what you are talking or writing about. In essence, when you tell a person something three times in a short theme, you are in danger of "hitting him over the head" or of leading him to believe that you really don't have much to say but keep repeating yourself to get three hundred or so words down on paper.

This is not to say, however, that you cannot use repetition in a theme. If you feel strongly about your topic, if you wish to give the impression that you know what you are talking about and have devoted long, hard thought to it, the classic form may be just the thing to convince the reader of your sincerity and strong feeling about the matter. If you have any misgivings, however, about the form, you could use either the inductive form or the deductive form and still accomplish your purpose. If you are going to repeat yourself to have something to say for a conclusion, look at HOW TO CONCLUDE A THEME at the end of this book.

APPLICATION: Now study the suggestions and read the list of do's and don't's. Then read each theme, including the analysis given. As you read each theme, refer to the suggestions and the list to see how the theme has implemented them. Once you have a good idea of what to do, look at the suggested list of topics and decide what your topic will be. When you have written your first draft, recheck the suggestions to see if you have included everything.

SUGGESTIONS: In the first paragraph, tell the reader what you are going to write about. Mention the major points of each paragraph which follows. Note that this development is very often used in speeches.

Tell the reader point 1 in the second paragraph. Begin by saying "My first point . . ." or with some such expression. Tell the reader point 2 in the next paragraph. Use the same type of beginning as you used in the second paragraph. Each subsequent point should have a separate paragraph.

Conclude by telling the reader what you told him. Repeat your main points, either exactly or in paraphrase. Use words like "therefore," "because of," etc., for emphasis.

DO'S AND DON'T'S:

1. Remember that to tell the reader something three times in a short paper makes for a rather tedious theme. The classic form is best used in speeches, long papers, term papers, involved presentations which are filled with many facts, figures, quotations, and the like. In long papers, in other words, your repetition is not so obvious.

2. If you must use the classic form in short themes, reserve it for arguments, sales talks, etc., where you want to stress sincerity, strong emotion, fixed conviction, and so on.

3. If you "tell me three times," rephrase your second and third telling; that is, say what you have said in your first paragraph in a different way. Again, remember how offensive television commercials are because of monotonous repetition.

4. Don't use the classic form for light, gay, inconsequential writing. Its very nature is one of firmness, sincerity, strong emotion, fixed conviction.

5. Using the classic form in short themes frequently gives evidence that a student's thinking is limited, that he is repeating himself to fulfill his quota of words. Teachers receiving this type of paper also frequently note faint pencil markings where the student has desperately counted his words.

6. The classic form is but an extension of DEDUCTIVE development. Most deductive themes tell the reader twice, but a theme which tells the reader each point only once is also quite common. See also INDUCTIVE.

7. Check the PROOFREADING CHART.

SAMPLE THEME—CLASSIC:

Is College Necessary?

In my opinion, college is very essential in today's society. Many reasons can be given for making such a statement, but to me the reasons are these: I can make more money with a college degree. I will be a better person with a college degree. When I receive a college degree, I will get to know people whom I have always admired.

The salaries earned by college graduates are better than the salaries earned by non-college people. Study after study has proved this point. In our society where achievement rightly or wrongly is measured by wealth, the ambitious person is faced with the choice of making himself a self-made success— this type of individual is becoming rare—or he can prepare himself for a career which rewards him with a high salary. The handwriting is on the wall: prepare or perish. I do not wish to perish.

My second reason is that I will be a better person with a college degree. I do not seek money alone. I seek experience that will aid in my intellectual and spiritual growth. I seek a diversity of experiences, of opportunities, of all those things one can find in college. In short, I will specialize in my field because of my interest and because it will afford me a good job, but I will also diversify as much as possible so that I do not become a person with a one-track mind.

My last reason, to get to know people whom I admire, is just as important to me as the other two reasons. While attending college a person makes friends and learns valuable lessons. He learns that "birds of a feather flock together"—that interesting, successful, and intelligent people attract one another in college and out of college. I have always admired my father and his friends—lawyers, judges, business and professional men. I want to be like them and to be with them. Thus, preparing myself for a career in business will one day assure me that I will be a businessman.

In brief, money, experiences, and friends are the three words that have sent me to college and are the three words which will keep me here until I graduate.

ANALYSIS: This theme is a legitimate use of the classic development in that the author is sincere and wishes to convince us by repeating his major points. He does not waste words in his introduction, but rather gets immediately to the point. This no-nonsense directness is in keeping with his development.

Then, in paragraphs two, three, and four, he wisely puts his topic sentence first in each paragraph. Again, this is a positive, direct approach. We may disagree with his reasons, but they are his reasons, and his details are adequate for the development of the theme.

The short conclusion is also in keeping with the no-nonsense tone. It leaves the reader with the feeling that the author knows what he wants and is willing to work for it.

SAMPLE THEME—CLASSIC:

My Impressions of College

I am constantly being asked how I like college. When I go home on weekends, many of my friends still in high school want to talk about college. Here is what I tell them. The school is too big; the teachers seem to feel that students are in the way; and the town distrusts all students.

What do I mean by saying that the school is too big? Well, the punched cards seem to be more important than the human beings they represent. To the Registrar I am nothing but a number. One of my teachers has us put our I.D. numbers on our papers instead of our names. He says that it is more objective, that he won't know who is who until he averages up the final grade. The class is too huge. How can I learn history when I'm the sixth person in the twentieth row? Then, too, we have only eight minutes between classes. It is impossible to get from my class in the Agriculture Building to the third floor of Old Main in less than twelve minutes. My dormitory is sixteen minutes away from Old Main. And Fraternity Row is even farther away from Old Main. Use a bicycle? There are so many bicycles crowding the roads and the bicycle racks that little time is saved in getting from place to place.

Secondly, the teachers' attitude is very cold. We are supposed to have a top-rated faculty, but I haven't seen any in my classes. One of my teachers will see students only before or after class, never in his office. He as much as told us that he is bored with us, that students are of secondary importance on campus. I have gone to see my mathematics teacher twice, but he is never in his office. If some of our "top-rated" faculty could hear what is said about them, they would start selling shoes.

And last, the town exists to prey on the students. It is impossible to cash a check in town. The police seem to live on the streets around the campus, writing tickets as fast as they can. All the new parking meters way out here are strictly a way to get money. Making the students who live in town buy a sticker is another graft. And the rooming-house owners have all gotten together to charge ten dollars a week for a room, no matter how many live in the room.

So, because of the size of the school, the attitude of the teachers, and the way the town treats us, I have to be honest whenever anyone asks me what I think of the school. I tell them that I don't like it. I am going to transfer to a smaller, friendlier school next year and finish my education there.

ANALYSIS: This theme is also a legitimate use of the classic development. The author could have used the DEDUCTIVE form of development, but since he feels so strongly about his subject, he has decided to reinforce his strong feelings by repeating his points.

In paragraphs two, three, and four, the author gives enough details to back up his disliking the college. We might argue that his reasons could be wrong, that he is in error about the college, yet to him they are adequate reasons. Note also the wise use of qualifying words—"seem" in two places— where a broad condemnation would be too strong.

The conclusion is very good. It restates the author's main points and enforces his tone of sincerity by telling us that he intends to do something about the situation.

SUGGESTED TOPICS FOR CLASSIC THEMES:

1. The Necessity for College

2. Our Declining Moral Standards

3. The Forgotten Student

4. Do We Need Subsidized Athletes?

5. Let's Get Behind Our Team

6. The Student's Right to Choose His Teachers

7. Equal Pay for Equal Work

8. TV Rating Systems Must Go

9. Discrimination Must End

10. Why Car Insurance Is Necessary

CLASSIFICATION

A classification theme is not difficult to write. The development you choose will probably be DEDUCTIVE. In the first paragraph, tell the reader how you would classify something—students, teachers, girls, boys, etc.—or how something is classified by textbooks, authorities, or others: roofing materials, animals, major crimes, reading material, woods, etc. The former is your own classification and can be written without research. The latter requires the use of printed authorities; usually textbooks or trade manuals, government publications, or similar materials.

If you are writing your personal classification, be careful not to choose too broad a subject. Don't, for instance, try to classify "students." Instead, classify "Three kinds of students who share my dormitory room." Choose "Three dogs I have owned" over "Dogs." Choose "My Clothing" over "Clothing." In short, limit your classification.

If you choose a traditional classification, do not plagiarize. That is, you are permitted to use a textbook classification, but not the author's words or sentences unless you use quotations.

The question to ask is this: Does this theme sound like me or like a textbook?

APPLICATION: Now study the suggestions and read the list of do's and don't's. Then read each theme, including the analysis given. As you read each theme, refer to the suggestions and the list to see how the theme has implemented them. Once you have a good idea of what to do, look at the suggested list of topics and decide what your topic will be. When you have written your first draft, recheck the suggestions to see if you have included everything.

SUGGESTIONS: The development of a classification theme is often DEDUCTIVE. State your generalization in an introductory paragraph—how you or others classify your topic—and then discuss each category in separate paragraphs.

Use a separate paragraph for each division of your classification. Use any logical approach—chronological, increasing or decreasing importance, causal relationship, and so on—that best fits your topic. Be sure to continue with the type of development that your introduction and the paragraphs above have begun.

Most factual classifications (as found in textbooks) end quickly. That is, once the classification is over, stop. An original classification needs a conclusion.

DO'S AND DON'T'S:

1. Narrow your topic. For instance, rather than write about "College Teachers," limit your paper to three or four kinds of teachers.

2. If you are to write about only two classes, choose the COMPARE AND CONTRAST method.

3. Decide whether you want to write a factual classification (one that authorities have already agreed upon) or a personal classification (original plan with you). See the list of suggested topics.

4. If it is a personal classification, use a logical division. Also,

do not attempt complete coverage. Use QUALIFIERS (See DEFINITIONS).

5. Do not overlap classifications. That is, make sure that a thing belonging to one class does not also belong to another class. For instance, if you classify automobiles as Imported, Expensive, and Economical, you will find that some automobiles belong to more than one class.

6. Do not over-generalize. That is, do not try to force everything into three or four categories. All students, for example, cannot be forced into three or four categories. Again, see QUALIFIERS and DEFINITIONS.

7. Your knowledge of outline procedure will be of value in determining which points are major and which are minor. Thus, each paragraph will deal with a major classification (the topic sentence), but it will also discuss minor divisions of the classification. Also, if your classification involves a number of categories, a preliminary outline will save you much time in writing your paper.

8. Check the PROOFREADING CHART.

SAMPLE THEME—TRADITIONAL CLASSIFICATION:

How Weaves Are Classified

Woven fabrics are made by the interlacing of two or more sets of yarn at right angles to produce a fabric. The length-wise yarn is called the warp, and the crosswise yarn is called the filling (woof). The three basic weaves are called plain, twill, and satin. Many interesting effects can be created by variations in these basic weaves.

The plain weave is the simplest and most inexpensive to manufacture. The filling and warp yarns interlace alternately, forming a plain weave which is durable and used often because it is suitable for most fibers. Sheeting and wooling broadcloth are two examples of plain-weave fabric.

There are variations in the plain weave which make fabric

more attractive. A ribbed or corded effect may be obtained by using filling yarns that are heavier than the warp yarns, or vice versa. The decorative blanket weave commonly used in oxford shirting is another variation of the plain weave. Here, one or more filling yarns is passed alternately over and under two or more warp yarns.

The twill weave is characterized by diagonal ridges formed by yarns which are exposed on the surface. Twill weaves are more closely woven, heavier, and sturdier than plain weaves. Gabardine, denim, and cotton twill are examples of twill weave fabric. Variations of the twill weave may be used to form herringbone or diamond patterns in the fabric.

The satin weave is really a broken twill, but the interlacings of the warp and filling yarns are spaced to avoid the formation of a wale or twill. The satin weave produces smooth, lustrous, rich looking fabric that gives reasonably good service. Fabrics of the satin weave are more appropriate for dress or formal wear because they are not so durable as fabrics of plain and twill weaves. Variations of the satin weave may be used to make a softer, less lustrous fabric. Examples of fabrics made in the satin weave are antique satin, bridal satin, and dress satin.

ANALYSIS: This is a good theme based upon a traditional classification. Note that such a classification means that it is already agreed upon by everyone. Thus, the author's task is largely one of taking the classification and presenting it in his own words and in logical order.

Paragraphing is not difficult in a traditional classification. Here, the author chose a topic which had three or four divisions and gave enough details to explain why the divisions were made.

Note also that the tone is strictly one of giving simple, clear, direct information. There is no need in such a discussion to entertain, to strive for eye-catching wording, or the like. The presentation of facts in a straightforward manner is the dominant intention.

SAMPLE THEME—PERSONAL CLASSIFICATION:

My Classification of Books

Books may be classified in many different ways, and most people would classify specific books in more than one category. In this paper I will attempt only to show my personal feelings as to how most books are grouped.

First, there are those books that are read because of their past literary importance and because of their value to those people interested in improvement or in enjoyment. Most of these books are important enough for a person to be considered not really well educated unless he has read them. Many of them contain information that applies to modern times as well as to the past. The Greek and Latin writers, Shakespeare, and various other books are examples of this first group.

The second group includes books that are important because of their technical or their special information. Textbooks, books pertaining to specialized occupations, and reference books fit into this group. These books are generally read less than those in the first group, but they are studied more carefully when they are read.

The third group of books includes those that are read partly for pleasure and partly for knowledge. This group might include better novels, semi-technical books, and many books which are labelled "light reading." These are the books which are read when enjoyment is the main objective.

The fourth and last group is made up of those books that contain very little information of any value. Their main topic is usually based on sensationalism, on scandal, on sex, and the like, and their selling point is loudly shouted. Such books do more harm than good.

Each person must choose the type of book which he likes and enjoys. Classification is usually an individual matter. But it must be obvious that the type of books one regularly reads is indicative of his personality. Thus, we college students may frequently complain about forced reading, but only in this way will many of us learn that we have too long contented ourselves with books included in the fourth group.

ANALYSIS: In this theme we have the author's own classification, not one traditionally accepted (see the previous theme). Thus the author wisely introduces his paper by using phrases like "may be" and "my personal feelings."

Note that this theme has a logical development. Obviously the author could have used many other forms. But, having made his choice, the problem then became one of making the writing interesting. In paragraphs two, three, four, and five, he does this by giving sufficient details to show that his classification is valid for his purpose.

The conclusion is good in that it repeats the idea that each of us can classify books as he wishes. The additional thoughts in the conclusion are good, but the author could have omitted them without hurting the theme.

SUGGESTED TOPICS FOR CLASSIFICATION THEMES:

1. Careers My Major Can Lead To

2. Divisions in My Major Department

3. TV Programs

4. Figures of Speech

5. The Popular Curriculum in Education

6. Dormitory Types

7. Show Dogs

8. Musical Instruments

9. Wild Game

10. Sporting Guns

COMPARE AND CONTRAST

A compare-and-contrast theme implies that you will present two things to the reader—two cars, two teachers, two vacation spots—and that you will discuss their good and bad points in relation to each other. The essence of such a presentation is that you or the reader will look at all the facts or issues involved and then make a choice about which is better.

In most cases, avoid an argumentative approach with equal items—two guns, for instance. That is, do not try to prove that one gun is better than another when both are popular makes, cost and perform the same, etc. You can compare and contrast the two, but unless your facts warrant otherwise, remain fair. In short, you may choose one over the other, but do not try to destroy the one you have not chosen. If you intend to prove that X is far better than Y, turn to the argument section and follow the directions given.

Remember also that choices fall into two categories: those made on the basis of logical thinking and those which are the result of whimsy or "flipping the coin"—choices, for example, about favorite foods, clothes, guns, etc. You can, then, where appropriate, "flip a coin" in your theme and prefer one thing over another on that basis.

APPLICATION: Now study the suggestions and read the list of do's and don't's. Then read each theme, including the analysis given. As you read each theme, refer to the suggestions and the list to see how the theme has implemented them. Once you have a good idea of what to do, look at the suggested list of topics and decide what your topic will be. When you have written your first draft, recheck the suggestions to see if you have included everything.

SUGGESTIONS: Compare-and-contrast themes usually take one of two forms (I refer to them as Form 1 and Form 2). The development of either form is essentially DEDUCTIVE or INDUCTIVE; Form 1 is more common.

Form 1: discuss all of one thing. You could use one paragraph for all the good, and one for all the bad. Then discuss all aspects of the second item. Follow the paragraphing of the first item. If you are discussing more than two major points, see DEFINITION form.

Form 2: discuss point 1 of A and B. Point out both similarities and differences. Then discuss point 2 of A and B. Each succeeding paragraph will discuss another point of A and B. If there are many points, use Form 1.

In your conclusion for either form, you may or may not decide in favor of one. If you intend to say that A is better than B, see also ARGUMENT development.

DO'S AND DON'T'S:

1. Form 1 is called opposing pattern; form 2, alternating.

2. In a short paper, restrict the comparison and contrast. That is, tell the reader that you are going to compare and contrast two things, not everything. If you are going to compare and contrast three or more things, see the DEFINITION-ANALYSIS form.

3. Things compared and contrasted must be logically related. They must be alike and, of course, different. Weighing the evidence and choosing among alternatives are both involved.

4. Handle both sides in the same manner. The essence of comparing and contrasting is fairness.

5. Mere order is not sufficient. You must impart your familiarity with and interest in the alternatives you are discussing.

6. If there will be many points to be compared and contrasted (for instance, country vs. city life), it is better to use Form 1. It is tedious to both writer and reader to be constantly switching back and forth (the alternating pattern).

7. Do not attempt too big a topic. If you do, you will be

forced into a series of platitudes or generalities which will give you organization without interest.

8. Remember that since you are comparing two things, you will use the comparative degree of adjectives. One thing will be bigger, smaller, taller, costlier, better, more nearly perfect, more nearly round, etc., than another. The superlative degree (biggest, smallest, tallest, costliest, best, etc.) is used when comparing three or more things.

9. Check the PROOFREADING CHART.

SAMPLE THEME—COMPARE AND CONTRAST (Form 1):

Advantages and Disadvantages of Being a Married Student

Marriage seems to give many people in college a determination to succeed that is quite often not found in the unmarried student. Perhaps the responsibility of having another person to consider besides himself motivates the married student to work harder. Many times married students must depend upon themselves for at least part of their livelihood. This helps them to realize the expense of a college education, and also how important it is to have this education.

Statistics do prove that fewer married students meet with failure in college. However, it might be important at this point to consider the type of person who will continue college after marriage. Most married students live in semipoverty. These same students could provide their families with at least a few luxuries if they were willing to accept any sort of available position. Instead, they are willing to wait and sacrifice in order to have a fuller life.

It is also noticeable that married students receive support and encouragement from friends and from teachers. The school also provides organizations and activities which furnish social outlets for the married students and their wives. In addition, many colleges make some sort of low-cost housing available for married students.

The above reasons, of course, are not all the advantages. But to me they are major advantages. Let us now look at some of the disadvantages of being married.

First of all, college is centered on the unmarried student. Most of the activities, the meetings, the stress placed upon being well-rounded is directed at the single student. Accordingly, the married student frequently finds himself left out of many of these experiences. The Rah-Rah aspect is thus very often not a part of a married student's experience. The Big Game, the Homecoming, the Big Dance of the year frequently find the married student absent.

Why is the married student frequently left out? The answer, of course, reveals one of the major disadvantages of being married while still in college—the financial hardship. Very often the married student must make drastic financial adjustments. Both he and his wife find themselves giving up almost all the luxuries they once took for granted. Social life is drastically curtailed, entertainment is minimal, clothing is worn long after it should have been discarded, and living quarters are frequently inferior. And if a third member of the family should come along, even further adjustments must be made.

Another disadvantage is that a person's interests change, and he finds himself no longer having anything in common with his old friends. Of course, new friends are made, but most of these new friendships are only temporary; the saying that "Misery loves company" expresses why such friendships are sought.

So I must conclude that being a married college student has its ups and downs. Gone for awhile are the good times and the carefree fun. But in their place come an increased maturity, an increased desire to succeed, and increased motivation to graduate. Whether the advantages outweigh the disadvantages is a question that each individual must decide for himself.

ANALYSIS: This theme is a good example of looking at both sides of a topic. Note that the author does not try to force the reader to agree with him, but instead uses words like "seems" and "perhaps." Thus, we cannot say that he generalizes too much or that he uses faulty logic.

In keeping with his title, the author first discusses what to him are advantages. Then, he has a good transitional paragraph (number four) to switch to his discussion of the disadvantages. A transition of some sort is mandatory in any compare-and-contrast development. Note also that the author could have used many more details had he chosen to do so.

The concluding paragraph is very good in that it repeats the thought that each of us must decide for himself, that each of us must consider his own point of view and circumstances. Had the author tried to make us decide in favor of one side or the other, he would have had great difficulty in writing the theme.

SAMPLE THEME—COMPARE AND CONTRAST (Form 2):

Open-faced or Closed-faced?

My title may be momentarily misleading, but it is accurate. What it means is that I have a problem deciding which fishing reel to buy, an open-faced or a closed-faced model. Terminology changes, even in fishing, and a few years ago the open-faced reel was called a "spinning" reel and the closed-faced reel was called a "spin-cast" reel. However, there was and is so much confusion about the names that many manufacturers now settle on "open" and "closed." The open-faced reel hangs below the rod; the closed-faced reel sits on top of the rod. Also, the open-faced reel has the line visible; the closed-faced has a cover over the line.

Both reels are good. Both of them use monofilament line, which has low visibility and is inexpensive. Both reels practically eliminate backlash, or "bird's-nest"—meaning a tangled line which was the curse of the older casting reels. And both reels are in the same price range so that, dollar for dollar, one cannot go wrong in buying either.

But there are differences. First of all the open reel is about six to eight inches long. It hangs below the rod, catches on brush when I walk along the bank, and is rather awkward looking. The closed reel is compact, perhaps four inches high, fits snugly on the rod, and is streamlined. We fishermen are just as concerned about beauty as anyone; so the appearance has to be considered.

Changing lines is a bit easier on the open reel. All one has to do is loosen a wing nut, slide off the old spool, and put on a new spool. One does the same with the closed reel, but first one has to remove the cover by loosening a screw which holds it in place. For a fisherman in a hurry, this process takes another minute or two. Sometimes seconds are precious to a fisherman.

The open reel is a bit more awkward to fish with. It has a bail, a device which one has to flip each time he casts. In short casting over long periods of time, it becomes a nuisance. The closed reel, on the other hand, is controlled entirely by the thumb lever, a device which is handy, quick, and instinctively used.

The open reel has two other faults. Because it hangs below the rod, one has to buy a special straight rod for it. The closed reel, on the other hand, can fit on any casting rod (one with the handle slightly offset). There are special "spin-casting" rods one can buy, but any casting rod from four to seven feet can be used. And, because I am left-handed, I have to buy the left-handed model of the open reel. Naturally enough, there aren't many models to choose from. We lefties, however, use the regular model of the closed reel, and we have many dozens of models to choose from.

And so, considering all the possibilities, I have a problem. Eventually, I hope to own both types. But I can assure you that I am not worried; I have had a wonderful time looking at catalogs, trying reels, and talking to people who own both. Choosing equipment, in other words, is just as enjoyable to me as using it once I purchase it.

ANALYSIS: Like the previous theme, this theme is wisely developed along the lines of presenting the facts and leaving the decision to the reader. It is much better for a young writer to have this approach than it is for him to try to convince the reader that one thing is much better than the other.

Note that while we have many details in this theme, the author has chosen the alternating pattern. He could just as easily have chosen the contrasting pattern (discussing all the details about the open-faced first, and then all the details about the closed-faced reel).

Also note that the author had to make an outline before he wrote the theme. The main consideration was a logical, orderly development that did not omit any important considerations. When there are many details to be considered and discussed, an outline is of considerable help in organizing one's thoughts.

SUGGESTED TOPICS FOR COMPARE-AND-CONTRAST THEMES:

1. High School and College

2. My Two Friends

3. Two Kinds of Teachers

4. Automatic Drive and "Four on the Floor"

5. Educational and Commercial TV

6. How I Turned A Failing Year into A Passing Year

7. Expensive and Inexpensive Hobbies

8. Science and the Arts

9. The Double Barrel and the Automatic Shotgun

10. Foreign and American Cars

DEDUCTIVE

The deductive development is the most common form used in writing expository themes because it follows basically the way we think and talk. A child says, "I don't like you because you're mean and nasty." This, in essence, is the deductive form: a generalization, "I don't like you," followed by the particulars, "because you're mean and nasty." Thus, any statement followed by reasons is a deductive statement.

In a theme of three hundred words or so, we develop each of the specific points in separate paragraphs. "Mean" and "nasty" in the child's statement would thus become the topic sentences of two separate paragraphs. You have a choice of giving all the reasons in your first paragraph and repeating each reason as you develop it in a subsequent paragraph, or of just stating the generalization in your first paragraph and then discussing each reason in each of the following paragraphs. If you wish to go further and repeat the details a third time, see CLASSIC development. If you wish to save your generalization (the thesis sentence) for the end of your theme, see INDUCTIVE development. For a more detailed discussion of how to write the deductive form, read TO THE STUDENT at the front of this book.

APPLICATION: Now study the suggestions and read the list of do's and don't's. Then read each theme, including the analysis given. As you read each theme, refer to the suggestions and the list to see how the theme has implemented them. Once you have a good idea of what to do, look at the suggested list of topics and decide what your topic will be. When you have written your first draft, recheck the suggestions to see if you have included everything.

SUGGESTIONS: State the topic and the generalization in the opening paragraph. No matter what the topic, it can be broken into logical parts. Each paragraph which follows discusses each part in turn. Remember that neither your title nor your thesis sentence is part of your theme. You must, therefore, state your topic in this paragraph.

The second paragraph deals with the first part of your topic, which becomes your topic sentence of the paragraph. See DEFINITIONS. The third paragraph discusses the second part of your topic, which becomes your topic sentence of the paragraph. Each succeeding paragraph will discuss another major point of your topic. Use the same type of beginning used in the paragraphs above.

See HOW TO CONCLUDE A THEME in the appendix. It is acceptable to repeat your major points in the conclusion. See also CLASSIC form.

DO'S AND DON'T'S:

1. The deductive form is by far the most common development used in themes. Unless specifically instructed otherwise, all your themes could take this development.

2. Be sure to state your thesis (see DEFINITIONS) early, preferably in the first paragraph. The conclusion could restate the thesis. See CLASSIC form.

3. If you are writing an Argument, be sure to check the ARGUMENT section.

4. If you wish to "hold off" your topic until the conclusion, see INDUCTIVE form.

5. Remember that a new paragraph is a signal to the reader that you are going to discuss another point.

6. You can arrange your points so that the most important ones come last, or in chronological order, or in causal order, or in any logical order.

7. For varied ways to begin paragraphs, see "Transition" in the DEFINITIONS included in the appendix. Also check number 11 in the PROOFREADING CHART.

8. Go over your theme for the specific suggestions made in the PROOFREADING CHART.

SAMPLE THEME—DEDUCTIVE:

Why I Hunt with a Muzzle Loader

Black-powder, or muzzle-loading, guns were the weapons of our forefathers and are becoming more and more popular among the sportsmen of America. There are many reasons for this popularity. In this paper, I shall explain why I have taken up the hobby of using a muzzle loader.

With the ever-increasing cost of modern guns and ammunition, the black-powder gun offers to any man with the patience to load and care for his weapon an excellent opportunity for economy. The price per shot of a muzzle loader is under three cents; the price per shot with a modern gun is between eight and twenty cents, depending upon the brand, the caliber, and the like.

Conservation laws in many states have been changed to allow an early season on big game which is open only to archers and to muzzle loaders. The reason for this is that since it is more difficult for these hunters to stalk and kill their game than it is for the hunters with modern guns, some advantage should be given. Also, in the case of the archer and the muzzle loader, since only one shot can be made and the hunter knows it must count, there are fewer wild shots, other hunters are in less danger, and less game is slightly wounded to wander off and die a slow death.

There is a certain thrill which goes with shooting an antique weapon, something above the feeling that a hunter with a modern weapon has. Once again, hunting becomes a challenge rather than a simple routine of walking into the woods with a weapon which will shoot accurately for great distances and of killing an animal that is almost out of sight to the naked eye. Even when I am stalking a squirrel, I almost expect a man in buckskin breeches and coonskin cap to step from behind a tree and inquire how my luck is going.

And then there is the thrill of the recognition we muzzle loaders get from other hunters. After the hunt I like to join a party of hunters—with my powder horn and bullet pouch hanging from my shoulder and my long barreled, black-powder rifle in my hand—and watch the expression on the faces of the jokers suddenly change when they see that my game bag is bulging. Yes, the hunters with their expensive equipment are forced to admit that a hunter with old-fashioned equipment is probably a better sportsman and a more pleased sportsman than they are. What more can any outdoorsman ask than to be recognized as a true sportsman?

ANALYSIS: The deductive development in this theme is entirely logical. The title and the introductory paragraph give us the general topic, and then paragraphs two, three, four, and five have the particulars. Note that paragraph three discusses the longer hunting season and the humane aspects. The two topics are closely related and thus can be combined, although the author could have logically made a separate paragraph for the latter discussion.

Note that the final paragraph effectively combines the author's fourth reason and his conclusion. Note also that his fourth reason is to him the most important reason. Since all of his particulars are about equal in importance, it became just a matter of choice which he chose to emphasize.

SAMPLE THEME—DEDUCTIVE:

The Lingering Past

In this day of modernity, space exploration, fast living, and rapid transportation, remnants of the last century linger. About ten miles north of Highway 90 where it enters Davis County near Cooperstown, there is an area which contains much of nineteenth-century life. These remnants are evident in the buildings and in the practices found there. I would like to tell you something about the area.

There are many relics which tell of the past. Near a place called Shallows of the Brambles, on the Brambles River, is an early nineteenth-century blast furnace. This furnace is perhaps the oldest building in the area. Not too far from this furnace are the remains of a Civil War hospital and of a powder mill. The powder mill used the power obtained from the water of Maple Creek on which it is located. About a dozen miles from Maple Creek is the community known as Hampeth. It boasts a log cabin which is at least one hundred and fifty years old and which is still being lived in. The cabin is in a hollow, and about twenty yards away are the traces of an old stage road which was once traveled by the circuit riders.

If we look at a map, we can see that Hampeth is only about twenty miles from the state capital. Yet, electricity did not come to Hampeth until after World War II! Even today, many of the people still use kerosene lamps and wood stoves. Gravel roads wind in and around the hills and, more often than not, one will come across horse drawn wagons. The road in many places dips down to go through the creek, not over it on a bridge. In fact, until a few years ago, the main road through the area was the creek bed. Even now, the gravel road follows the creek through the county.

And how do these people make a living? Many of the men still trap and sell furs. Until the bounty was removed, many a man made a few dollars by hunting foxes. A patch of ground, a few hogs, a few scraggly chickens, and perhaps a small still hidden off in a patch of thicket—from these, the people eke out their living.

And there are two institutions still operating which are remnants of the past. One is the church. It is an ancient wooden building, made from the trees in the area, and it is a perfect example of a community church. At Christmas the children have the traditional pageant; a Christmas tree is cut from the nearby woods, and Santa Claus comes with his bag of presents. The church is heated with a wood-burning stove, but the spirit of friendliness and love is still as strong as it was a hundred years ago.

The other institution is the general store. It looks exactly like the old general stores in advertisements. It is a combination grocery, post office, hardware, farm supply, barber shop. The men gather around its wood-burning stove and chew tobacco and tell lies as their forefathers did. It is still the one most popular gathering spot in the community.

Thus, even though the world advances and life becomes more hectic every day, the past still lingers in Hampeth. And who would change it? I for one love this region and its people, and I would not change it for all the world.

ANALYSIS: As is correct for a deductive development, the author states a generalization in the first paragraph—he is going to discuss an area that has many features of the previous century. Then, in subsequent paragraphs, the author describes individual particulars as evidence of his generalization. As was necessary for the previous theme, the author had to organize his particulars before writing. Thus, paragraph two discusses the old buildings; paragraph three, primitive conditions and roads; paragraph four, the economic life; and paragraphs five and six, two institutions. The arrangement is the author's choice; he could have rearranged these paragraphs in any fashion, just so long as they remained orderly. Note that paragraph two could have been made into two paragraphs and that paragraphs five and six could have been combined.

The conclusion is short and what we would expect the author to say; yet, note that the theme calls for such a concluding thought.

SUGGESTED TOPICS FOR DEDUCTIVE THEMES:

1. Three Types of Students

2. How to Study

3. Why I Came to College

4. People I Admire

5. My Goals in Life

6. Are College Students "Sheep"?

7. Why I Pledged

8. TV Wastelands

9. Why the Military Draft is Necessary

10. My Ambitions

(See also the topics suggested in the HOW-TO, ARGUMENT, and INDUCTIVE sections.)

DEFINITION-ANALYSIS

Definition and analysis are really two methods of explaining the same topic. When we define, we make something distinct, we explain it, we set it in a class by pointing out its characteristics. When we analyze, we break a thing up into its parts and show why each part fits into the whole. Thus, we can define what a dictionary is, or we can analyze the various functions of a dictionary; we can define what an internal combustion engine is, or we can analyze how the engine works. Thus, no matter what approach we may take, we can use both definition and analysis. Definition, in short, tells us what a thing is; analysis tells us why and how it is constructed.

As in the CLASSIFICATION development, we can either use our own personal definition or analysis, or we can discuss how authorities define and analyze something. Therefore, you are advised to turn to the classification section and read the introductory page. The same rules and cautions apply for a theme of definition or analysis.

APPLICATION: Now study the suggestions and read the list of do's and don't's. Then read each theme, including the analysis given. As you read each theme, refer to the suggestions and the list to see how the theme has implemented them. Once you have a good idea of what to do, look at the suggested list of topics and decide what your topic will be. When you have written your first draft, recheck the suggestions to see if you have included everything.

SUGGESTIONS: There is no set pattern for a theme which defines or analyzes. Once you have jotted down your ideas, arrange them in a logical order. You will discover that various developments, or a combination of developments, can be used. Suggested forms are DEDUCTIVE, INDUCTIVE, AND COMPARE-AND-CONTRAST.

A simple form of development is to state in one paragraph what a thing is (its definition). Then, in the following paragraph, you could say what the thing is not. Or, if the thing under discussion can be broken down into kinds or types, you can devote a separate paragraph to each kind or type. A "wrap-up" conclusion may or may not be needed. See HOW TO CONCLUDE A THEME.

DO'S AND DON'T'S:

1. As mentioned, a theme which defines or analyzes can be developed using various methods. See ANALOGY, COMPARE AND CONTRAST, DEDUCTIVE.

2. No matter what your development, use many examples, details, and facts. The more information you include, the clearer will be your meaning.

3. Be sure to include what a thing is not. That is, point out how it differs from things with which it could be or often is confused.

4. Suggested ways to develop your theme include these: Break down the complex into the simple. Put something into its class. Show the origin, cause, history, and so on, of the thing under discussion; also show the result, effect, use, purpose, etc.

5. Make your definition or analysis broad enough to cover everything which falls into the class. If not, tell the reader what you are excluding and why you are excluding it.

6. Don't use the thing being defined or analyzed in your definition. For example, don't say that "a combat soldier is a soldier who combats."

7. Don't use terms which are as difficult or as abstract as the thing under discussion. Use simpler terms, more familiar objects, and the like, for your illustrations.

8. Avoid using "is when," "is where," "is how," when stating definitions. Follow the verb with a noun: A definition is the explanation of the meaning of a word.

9. Don't attempt too difficult a topic for a short theme. The

danger is that you will not be thorough enough or will try to cover too much by using platitudes, over-simplifications, and generalities. Stick with the concrete at first, the visible; avoid writing about abstractions like beauty, truth, culture, education, justice, and the like.

10. Check the PROOFREADING CHART.

SAMPLE THEME—DEFINITION:

Polonius Defines A Man's Rules of Conduct

When I was in high school, I memorized the famous passage in *Hamlet* where Polonius gives his son, Laertes, some advice prior to Laertes' returning to France. The advice is concerned with how a man, or perhaps better, a gentleman, should conduct himself. Here is my interpretation of Polonius' remarks.

First of all, a man should not speak until he has given due thought to the consequences, nor should he act impulsively. In short, think before acting and consider your words well before speaking.

Next, choose your friends wisely. Respect all men, but do not regard that all men are alike. Don't make friends with just everyone and anyone. But once you have made friends, be true to them and expect that they will be true to you.

Keep out of quarrels, but do not run away from a quarrel of honor. And, once in an argument, conduct yourself honorably and in such a manner that your opponent will not take you too lightly. Along with this precept, be willing to listen to everyone's opinion. Be careful, however, to whom you express your opinions.

In the matter of clothing, buy the kind of clothes that you can afford, but don't wear fantastic or gaudy clothing. Note what the men of rank and stature are wearing and follow their practice. Remember that the type of clothing often tells what the wearer is like.

One's financial status is important. Accordingly, do not borrow money. Neither should you lend money. To borrow or to lend is to lose friends. Also, he who borrows shows a lack of common sense in personal economy.

Finally, lacking any person after whom one can model oneself, the best advice is to follow your own upbringing, lessons learned, and character. In other words, if you are true to yourself, you will then treat other men as you wish to be treated.

ANALYSIS: This theme effectively fulfills the assignment of defining something. Even though the definition is not original with the student, he has done a good job in interpreting and putting Shakespeare's poetry into prose. The opening paragraph is good in that it tells us what the topic to be defined is: the proper conduct for a gentleman.

The order of paragraphs is determined by the topics as they are found in the original source. Note that the student has found six main points and thus wisely uses six short paragraphs to discuss them.

There is no concluding paragraph because one is not necessary. The author could, of course, have written a conclusion, perhaps to the effect that the advice is still good today, or that Polonius did not live up to his own wisdom in the remainder of the play, and so on.

SAMPLE THEME—DEFINITION:

A Military Map

A military map is a graphic representation of the earth's surface drawn to scale and used by the Department of the Defense. A military map shows features which we find on ordinary road maps (such as those handed out by service stations), and it also includes other information of a specialized nature. There are three types of military maps which are used the most often.

The first type of military map is the planimetric map, which is very much like the service station map. This map shows only the horizontal or flat position of the terrain. It includes manmade objects such as towns and roads, and natural features such as rivers, lakes, and streams.

The second type of military map is the topographic map, which not only shows planimetric features but also shows relief or variations in the earth's surface. The topographic map has grid lines and a sheet number so that a soldier will be able to know the exact location of himself or others. This type of map shows terrain features by various colors, such as black for manmade objects, blue for water, green for vegetation, brown for relief features, red for roads, and other colors for special information.

The third type of military map is the photomap, which is a reproduction of a photograph or photomosaic. This map also has grid lines and a sheet number, but it is usually printed in black and white. Colored maps, of course, can also be used.

Military maps do not include aeronautical or hydrographic charts. These charts are used by special forces of the armed services and not by the common soldier. These specialized maps also refer to air currents or to areas of water as much as they do to land features.

ANALYSIS: This is a straightforward, factual theme. The author begins immediately with a definition of a military map and then in three paragraphs discusses the three kinds. The development is thus deductive. The details given are sufficient for the reader to know the difference in the maps. No words are lost by the author in giving the details because the purpose of his definition is to give facts, not fancy.

The final paragraph is short, but is necessary so that the maps excluded can be mentioned. The whole theme is one of impersonal presentation and is in keeping with the material discussed.

Note that the author undoubtedly used a textbook in military science as his source. Such use of authoritative material is perfectly acceptable, just so long as the student puts the material into his own words.

SAMPLE THEME—ANALYSIS:

Why Friendship Cliques Are a Problem

One of the many problems that confront psychologists, teachers, parents, and students themselves is the presence of social cliques in many high schools and colleges. Psychologists have determined two main factors that cause these cliques to be a problem: the harm done to those considered by the clique to be unacceptable and the harm done to those members of the clique who do the excluding.

Perhaps the former of the above problems is the more injurious, since usually more people are excluded from than are included in these groups. Many students are excluded because some member of the group does not like them. This kind of exclusion causes hurt feelings as well as feelings of inferiority. Those rejected for any reason often experience a sense of not belonging and of loneliness. Students may also be excluded for other reasons—lack of money, lack of personal attractiveness, lack of good family, lack of personality. Often the person repulsed for such reasons cannot help feeling inferior, and serious personality problems are a possible result.

The second factor causing cliques to be considered a special problem is the harm done by the limitation of experiences placed upon the group members. The broadening experience of varied friendships is frequently denied the clique members. They are frequently barred from the enriching personalities of people outside the group. Neither are they free to enjoy the activities in which those outside the group participate. It may be argued that many groups enjoy several different types of activity. Upon examination, however, the argument is usually proven to be only partially true. Whatever the case, if a young person belongs to a group which excludes many students, snobbery is inevitable. A snob, say the psychologists, has as much of a mental problem as does the person who has been excluded. Feelings of inferiority or of superiority are but two sides of a similar problem.

Many solutions have been tried and suggested for the problem of school cliques. It is obvious that there will always be cliques, and that there will always be the problems caused by the cliques. Time may help the individual, and time may dissolve the clique, but other problems and other cliques are sure to come along.

ANALYSIS: This analysis of cliques could also be called a definition in that it does define what problems are caused. The development is DEDUCTIVE, with the thesis given in the introduction and the two problems discussed in the following two paragraphs.

The author has chosen to break his discussion into two logical categories: the harm done to those excluded, and the harm done to those doing the excluding. As such, though he does not discuss all the problems, he makes sure that he has covered the widest possible area in the briefest breakdown.

The short conclusion is both necessary and fitting. The author wisely does not suggest that anything much will ever be done to remedy the situation.

SAMPLE THEME—LITERARY ANALYSIS:

The writing of literary analyses is a subject unto itself and calls for extended rules, varied techniques, and skills beyond the scope of this book. The following poem and analysis are presented as illustrative of the analysis form, not of the exact way to analyze literature.

A Description of a City Shower

by Jonathan Swift

Careful observers may fortell the hour
(By sure prognostics) when to dread a shower,
While rain depends, the pensive cat gives o'er
Her frolics and pursues her tail no more.
Returning home at night, you'll find the sink   5
Strike your offended sense with double stink.
If you be wise, then go not far to dine;
You'll spend in coach-hire more than save in wine.
A coming shower your shooting corns presage,

Old aches throb, your hollow tooth will rage: 10
Sauntering in coffee-house is Dulman seen;
He damns the climate and complains of spleen.

Meanwhile the South, rising with dabbled wings,
A sable cloud athwart the welkin flings,
That swilled more liquor than it could contain,   15
And, like a drunkard, gives it up again.
Brisk Susan whips her linen from the rope,
While the first drizzling shower is borne aslope:
Such is that sprinkling which some careless quean
Flirts on you from her mop, but not so clean: 20
You fly, invoke the gods; then turning, stop
To rail; she singing, still whirls on her mop.
Not yet the dust had shunned the unequal strife,
But, aided by the wind, fought still for life,
And wafted with its foe by violent gust,   25
'Twas doubtful which was rain and which was dust.
Ah! where must needy poet seek for aid,
When dust and rain at once his coat invade?
Sole coat, where dust cemented by the rain
Erects the nap, and leaves a cloudy stain.   30

Now in contiguous drops the flood comes down,
Threatening with deluge this devoted town.
To shops in crowds the daggled females fly,
Pretend to cheapen goods, but nothing buy.
The Templar spruce, while every spout's abroach,   35
Stays till 'tis fair, yet seems to call a coach,
The tucked-up sempstress walks with hasty strides,
While streams run down her oiled umbrella's sides.
Here various kinds, by various fortunes led,
Commence acquaintance underneath a shed.   40
Triumphant Tories and desponding Whigs
Forget their feuds, and join to save their wigs.
Boxed in a chair the beau impatient sits,
While spouts run clattering o'er the roof by fits,
And ever and anon with frightful din   45
The leather sounds; he trembles from within.
So when Troy chairmen bore the wooden steed,
Pregnant with Greeks impatient to be freed
(Those bully Greeks, who, as the moderns do,

Instead of paying chairmen, run them through),   50
Laocoon struck the outside with his spur,
And each imprisoned hero quaked for fear.

Now from all parts the swelling kennels flow,
And bear their trophies with them as they go:
Filth of all hues and odours seem to tell   55
What street they sailed from, by their sight and smell.
They, as each torrent drives, with rapid force
From Smithfield, or St. Pulchre's shape their course,
And in huge confluence joined at Snow Hill ridge,
Fall from the conduit prone to Holborn Bridge.   60
Sweepings from butchers' stalls, dung, guts, and blood
Drowned puppies, stinking sprats, all drenched in mud
Dead cats and turnip-tops come tumbling down the flood.

An Analysis of "A Description of a City Shower"

On the surface "A Description of a City Shower" is a very
colorful and vivid picture of eighteenth-century London immediately before, during, and after a shower. If the reader looks
more closely, he finds that Swift is satirizing weather prophets,
certain specific types of city characters, heroic poetry, and the
filthiness of English towns. The poem consists of four stanzas
which describe consecutively the shower's being forecast by
certain signs: the shower's initial outburst, the shower's main
deluge, and the shower's aftermath.

The first stanza begins by stating that weather can be forecast
and gives substantiating examples in the succeeding ten lines.
A pensive cat, a stinking sewer, painful corns, an aching tooth,
and a complaining hypochondriac are listed as "sure" signs
of impending rain. Swift advises the reader in lines 7-8 that
dining across town where the wine is cheaper will be impracti-
cal should it rain. The loafer in lines 11-12 is representative
of many people in eighteenth-century England who felt it
stylish to constantly complain of "spleen"—meaning melancholy or low spirits.

In the second stanza the shower's initial outburst stirs up the
dust and plasters everything with mud. The rain cloud is
alluded to as a drunkard ready to vomit from too much drink.

A housewife retrieves her washing from the line, but not before it is sprinkled with rain. Swift satirizes the epic smile in lines 19-22. He uses the transitional word "such" and appropriate epic form, but with degrading and comic intent. In lines 23-26 Swift describes the stirring of dust by the shower's initial sprinkling and wind. Lines 27-30 reveal a "needy" poet with only one coat and it plastered with mud.

The full blast of the shower is described in the third stanza; it causes various reactions in different people. Splattered women pretend to shop, and a lawyer pretends to wait for a coach; both are merely utilizing shelter from the rain. A seamstress with tucked-up skirt wades through the wet streets. To save their wigs, even such bitter political enemies as Tories and Whigs stand together under the same shelter. In lines 43-52 Swift depicts the animosity between noblemen and common servants. By analogy, he refers to a dandy and his chair-men as the Greeks and Trojans in Homer's *Odyssey*. The dandy is frightened by noises because he fears the chair-men may rob or murder him. Swift compares the dandy's fear to that of the Greeks inside the wooden horse at the gates of Troy. The parenthetical matter in lines 49-50 suggests the eighteenth-century dandy's ill-treatment of his chair-men. Swift again satirizes the epic smile in lines 47-52. He derives his "Troy chairmen," Greeks and "Laocoon" from the *Odyssey* but again uses Homer's material in a degrading manner.

The fourth stanza, which concerns the aftermath of the shower, paints an unforgettable picture of the city's filthiness. The open gutters with their burdens of waste make a lasting impression upon the reader. The triplet in lines 61-63, with its Alexandrine in line 63, is a satirical jab at heroic prosody. The heroic couplet, the triplet, and the Alexandrine are associated with epics and other heroic poetry. Swift uses these exalted poetic forms but fills them with the filthiest, most offensive subject matter imaginable.

Swift accomplishes at least three things in his poem. He depicts the eighteenth-century English city's physical conditions so well that the reader can almost smell the drains. His epithets very adeptly enhance the reader's conception of the characters in the poem. And finally, he manages some very good satire on heroic prosody, especially in the concluding triplet of the last stanza.

ANALYSIS: In analyzing literature, one of the easiest approaches is to discuss points item by item as they are found in the original, and to merely interpret each point as it is being discussed. Such is the technique found in this essay. The technique is the tried-and-true method used by students for generations. Because it is so conventional, however, many teachers forbid their students to write such an analysis.

Aside from the conventionality, this theme does a good job of interpreting Swift's poem. Note that the poem is relatively clear and direct, with little of the symbolism and imagery one ordinarily finds in poetry. As such, it is easier to interpret than a highly symbolic work.

The paragraphs logically follow the stanzas of the poem. The concluding paragraph is excellent in that it summarizes three things accomplished by Swift and gives evidence of some original thinking and acute observation by the student.

SUGGESTED TOPICS FOR DEFINITION—ANALYSIS THEMES:

1. Printed Electric Circuits (needs research)

2. College Dropouts

3. A Good Teacher

4. A Well-adjusted Person

5. Student Unrest

6. The Cold War (needs research)

7. A Well-balanced Diet (may need research)

8. Progressive Education (needs research)

9. The Teen Market—A Billion Dollar Industry

10. A Happy Home

11. Why Are So Many People Coming to College?

12. What is Medicare? (needs research)

13. The Driver's Test (may need research)

14. Is Service in the Peace Corps Valuable to the Individual? (needs research)

15. Why Is Television so Poor?

DESCRIPTIVE

Since you are a beginning writer, it is best that you do not try to write a descriptive theme to evoke a response—one in which skillful use of figures of speech, words, details, and tone induces in the reader strong feelings. Instead, since logical, organized, clear writing is your aim, descriptions which are informative are likely to be more successful.

Thus, avoid trying to duplicate the descriptions found in novels, poetry, advertisements, and the like. Instead, strive for the factual, condensed, detailed presentation that you find in textbooks (biology, chemistry, mathematics) or in mail-order catalogs.

With descriptive themes, a preliminary outline is strongly urged. It need not be a formal outline, but merely a list of features which you feel are the main ones. Group like details together, using any logical approach. An automobile, for instance, could be discussed in terms of styling, engine, and performance. Once you have grouped like items, each group will become a paragraph in your theme. If you feel that one group of details is more important, save this paragraph for the end.

APPLICATION: Now study the suggestions and read the list of do's and don't's. Then read each theme, including the analysis given. As you read each theme, refer to the suggestions and the list to see how the theme has implemented them. Once you have a good idea of what to do, look at the suggested list of topics and decide what your topic will be. When you have written your first draft, recheck the suggestions to see if you have included everything.

SUGGESTIONS: The introduction will let the reader know if you are being informative or evoking a response. Most themes do the former. There is no formula for developing a descriptive theme. Suggestions are order of place, order of prominence, order of importance, front to back, and so on. If you are describing a person, consider appearance, habits, gestures, mannerisms, speech, voice, what others say about him, and so on.

Each succeeding paragraph will be devoted to the particular order you have chosen. Use transitions (see DEFINITIONS). Move to another detail in each paragraph. Be sure that each paragraph has a topic sentence or a controlling idea.

Your conclusion could reaffirm your opening statements, or it could be a value judgment. See HOW TO CONCLUDE A THEME for other possible endings.

DO'S AND DON'T'S:

1. Remember that any description (of a person or thing) can have a logical division of presentation. Decide what the main points of interest are. Each of these main points will then have at least one paragraph devoted to it.

2. Descriptive writing, you will note, is developed just as are DEDUCTIVE or INDUCTIVE themes.

3. Describing a thing is much easier than describing a person.

4. Adjectives and figures of speech (similes and metaphors) are very important in descriptions. Remember that your choice of details and your choice of words are a clue to your feelings; they will also provoke a feeling in the reader. Be careful about the connotations of descriptive words.

5. Use concrete, specific wording, not vague, abstract word-

ing. Does a frightened rabbit run, hop, flee, scuttle, scurry, or bound?

6. There is a difference between giving information and evoking a response. The latter is very difficult.

7. Study descriptions given in catalogs, advertisements, and the like, which treat of the same thing you are to describe. Note the use of comparatives and superlatives.

8. Remember that most descriptive themes are assigned to test your ability to organize, as well as to test your ability to use figurative language.

9. Avoid clichés. Be careful of the words you use after *like* and *as*. On the other hand, do not wrack your brain trying to write new imagery. Farfetched figures of speech are as bad as trite figures of speech.

10. Note that descriptions written by advertising people are not always grammatically correct. They use the superlative degree when they should use the comparative. They say "This is a better buy!" In your theme, you would have to finish such a sentence by adding "than the other product."

11. Check the PROOFREADING CHART.

SAMPLE THEME—DESCRIPTION:

Twenty Oaks

The boundaries of my childhood community were not easily defined, but the neighborhood children generally considered our domain to extend as far west as the village school and as far east as the country church just beyond the Moore's country estate, "Twenty Oaks." Here between these two boundaries, we managed to squeeze out of life all that a semiprogressive farming community would afford.

Our farm, "Walnut Grove," which looked about as undignified as its name sounds, was the halfway point between the two boundaries. The broad expanse of corn fields across the road from our house rose up to defeat me. To the west, extending from our farm almost to the school house, lay an area of unimpressive lowland.

Going eastward from our farm on one of the high flats, one could see the other farm houses sprinkled out on the hills or down in the flats between—the rolling hills and curving flats giving the whole countryside an appearance of a roller coaster all the way from Walnut Grove to Twenty Oaks.

Had it not been for Twenty Oaks, our place would not have looked so commonplace in comparison with most of the other farms, but compared to Twenty Oaks, it was nothing. For to me Twenty Oaks was the epitome of wealth and prestige. I would pause with a mingled sense of pride and envy before the long, winding, oak-lined driveway leading up to the iron fence surrounding the gleaming white mansion of the Moores. The huge white barn and the red and white windmill added to the picturesque effect. But it was the stately oaks, towering above the whole countryside, which aroused within me a burning ambition to attain the dignity and prestige synonymous with Twenty Oaks. Yes, the estate set my heart aglow with the dream that one day I would own it, that I could say "I have arrived!"

It was not that I really envied the Moores or coveted their estate. It was all that it stood for that challenged me and spurred me on. It was just that the Moore's way of life made mine seem drab by comparison. How well I remember the hot day when I was weeding our garden and the Moores went riding off on their vacation in Wisconsin!

As I look back, I believe that it was not so much the obvious wealth of Twenty Oaks that intrigued me and allured me as it was the feeling of importance and exhilaration I got from just passing by, or from those rare times when I walked down the long, winding drive, the oak leaves crunching under my feet, and the cool breeze blowing my hair. My steps would be slow, for I savored each inch of the way, and my emotions would spur me to dreaming that one day, I, the Lady of the House, would be waiting graciously on the wide and cool front porch to welcome the streams of friends who would be my guests.

ANALYSIS: This theme is obviously the work of a keen, perceptive student. The details are numerous and graphic, the descriptions are fresh and vivid, and the emotions felt by the author and reader are genuine. In short, the author's desire to evoke a response in her reader succeeds admirably.

Note that the paragraphing combines various forms of description. The first three paragraphs are concerned with the geography of the region. Paragraph four describes the estate. Paragraph five deals with the way of life of the owners of the estate. And the conclusion is concerned with the impressions formed in the mind of the author.

Note particularly the vocabulary used: domain, expanse, epitome, picturesque, and so on. By her choice of words the author has materially increased the effectiveness of her theme.

SAMPLE THEME—DESCRIPTION:

Faraway Places

My neighborhood was high adventure when I was a child. It was the challenge of a hike into the deep, black African forest or the excitement of a long voyage across an ocean. It was adventure because it was on the edge of town where only a few streets had cut through the pastures and only a few houses had broken the fields of knee-high grass. It was adventure because there were forests of weeds that were taller than a child, and because there was an ocean, or at least a pond that seemed like an ocean to me. This neighborhood always gave us something to do.

We never had to worry about what game to play next or what we would do tomorrow. In fact, we never had time to do all of the things we wanted to do. We never had enough time to play all the games, climb all the trees, ride all the horses, or build all the tree houses and hide-outs that we would have liked to. Summer went by rapidly, so rapidly that the time between Memorial Day and Labor Day was just a blur. And in the winter we never found enough time after school to do all of the ice skating, build all the snowmen, track all the wild rabbits, or play all the games in the snow that we wanted to.

The real adventure was in the places we went. The most exciting of these was Crow Creek, just down the gravel road around the curve, where a rickety old bridge spanned a creek about four feet wide, just where willowy trees cast their shade. Days would go by without any traffic on the road, and we children regarded the area as our private property. Nothing was more fun than sneaking away from home—our mothers were afraid of the snakes—cutting across the fields, and wading in the creek, fishing for minnows, skipping stones, and capturing frogs.

Next on our list of adventurous places was the Big Oak. It was in a field of high weeds far away from home and out of sight of the road. There we had our picnics, built our tree houses, hid our secret things, and played our games. Moreover, just down the road from the oak was our secret blackberry patch. It, too, was forbidden territory because of the snakes, but no child in our area missed the ripe berries, and no mother could be fooled when she saw the berry-stained lips and hands of the children.

And then it all came to an end! One day, bulldozers and trucks and men and all the other noise and dust of progress came. Sewer and water lines, electric and telephone wires, carpenters and plumbers and brick layers—soon our rural retreat became another subdivision. There isn't much left now to remember, except the names of the streets, fanciful names like Indianwood, Sunset, and Oak Lane. The latter street goes right by the only thing left once the bulldozers finished—our Big Oak tree.

ANALYSIS: As in the previous theme, the purpose here is to evoke a response. It succeeds quite well. The introduction is interestingly written with its promise to tell of the adventures of the children. The word choice is good, the details are sufficient, and the mood excellently portrays the excitement of the author both as an adult with memories and as a child actually living in the area.

The paragraphs logically focus upon the various play places that the children had. Obviously, paragraphs two, three, and four could easily be changed around.

The conclusion is excellent in that it adds a touch of pathos to what is a wide-eyed account of innocence. The last line is also a terse and appropriate detail. The theme, in short, is enjoyable.

SUGGESTED TOPICS FOR DESCRIPTIVE THEMES:

1. An Outdoor Paradise

2. A Beautiful Car

3. A College Town

4. What Tourists Want to See in My Home Town

5. The New Housing Project

6. What Is a Cow College?

7. A Farm Boy Visits the City

8. A Beautiful Vacation Spot

9. A Hotrod

10. My Home

11. My Dormitory Room

12. How Not to Teach

13. My Dream Husband

14. A Good Girlfriend

15. My Father

FLASHBACK

The flashback is a tried-and-true device to capture the reader's attention. Since the end of (or the reason for) any sequence of events is usually the most interesting, the flashback is used to hint at that end or reason. The flashback, thus, is not a development in itself, but is used in conjunction with other developments.

While the flashback is common in literary presentations—novels, dramas, television programs—it need not be restricted to them. Indeed, it is very often used for expository writing. The illustrative theme "Check Your Equipment" in this section is a valid expository use of the flashback technique. In paragraph four, the generalization "Check your fishing equipment" is followed by the particulars. The theme is thus DEDUCTIVE.

Flashbacks also can be and are used throughout a novel, play, movie, etc. But for a young writer, it is best to restrict its use to the beginning. The one thing to be careful of is that the flashback is not foolish, that it is in keeping with the purpose of the expository writing. In short, a flashback does not have to be literary or dramatic; it can be as matter-of-fact as the remainder of the theme. If it captures the reader's interest without causing him to laugh at the author, it succeeds.

APPLICATION: Now study the suggestions and read the list of do's and don't's. Then read each theme, including the analysis given. As you read each theme, refer to the suggestions and the list to see how the theme has implemented them. Once you have a good idea of what to do, look at the suggested list of topics and decide what your topic will be. When you have written your first draft, recheck the suggestions to see if you have included everything.

SUGGESTIONS: Begin a flashback as close to the conclusion, the effect, as you can. Do not "give the plot away" in the first paragraph, but end the paragraph with a question, with a comment that the remainder of the theme will pertain to the flashback. In a short theme, your flashback should be short, certainly no longer than about one-fourth of your theme.

The succeeding paragraphs will then follow a logical order, usually chronological, step-by-step, or ascending order of importance. In a paper of theme length, the flashback should not be too long, perhaps two paragraphs at the most. It is possible to use reverse chronology all through the paper. See CHRONO-LOGICAL form.

In a short theme, you should arrive at where you began your theme in about the fourth paragraph. Then finish your development. You may or may not have a concluding paragraph. In a long paper, you may continue with advice, a discussion of similar things, do's and don'ts and so on.

DO'S AND DON'T'S:

1. Note that the flashback form uses the cause-to-effect form in reverse. That is, all or part of the effect, the result, the conclusion, is given first; then you go back and trace the particulars, usually in chronological order.

2. The flashback technique is used frequently in hunting and fishing articles, adventure stories, how-to-do articles, and the like, as a rhetorical device to capture the reader's interest. It is also a frequent device in television and in the movies.

3. A good way to write a theme using the flashback is to write the theme using one of the usual forms. Then, write the flashback. In other words, you have to know your ending before you can write a flashback which hints at or gives the conclusion.

4. Since the flashback technique often involves action and dialogue, it should be considered for lighter veins, for drama, for literary effectiveness. It is best not to use it for serious subjects, highly scientific reports, and the like, where the reader's interest is not so much one of literary curiosity as it is in the subject itself. Thus, a report on the cause of the death of fish in a polluted stream would not use the flashback if it were for a scientific journal, but could use it in a popular magazine which sportsmen read.

5. Be sure that your flashback is effective, pertinent, valid, not just thrown in as an "arty" technique.

6. Check the PROOFREADING CHART.

SAMPLE THEME—FLASHBACK:

Check Your Equipment

"No more talking," I whispered to Billy. "Crawl real slow. Don't make any noise. Whatever you do, don't stand up." Billy nodded his head. He knew that it was now or never as well as I did. It was our last chance before striking camp and returning home.

The last twenty yards I covered as cautiously as a soldier crawling across a battlefield. And this was war, war against old "Bucket head," the name given to the huge bass that had set up his domain in the deep pool at the wide turn of the creek. Dozens of fishermen had tried to catch him; a few had managed to hook him, but the bass had darted around sunken logs and weeds so that the fishermen eventually pulled in a broken line. Now it was my turn. That is why my approach was so cautious. Just a few feet more remained until I reached the safety of the bush which would hide me from view of the bass.

Finally I reached the bush. I stood up slowly, looked to see if Billy was watching, and waved at him. My fly rod was already assembled. Three times I false cast, being careful that the live cricket on my hook would not be pulled off. Then, the final swing of the rod, with just a bit more pressure so that the hook would settle far out near the willow. And that's what undid me: the tip section of my flyrod came loose and went flying to land with a splash in the center of the pool. There went my chance to fool anything. After a splash like that, even the minnows would remain quiet for an hour.

Has something like this ever happened to you? Of course it has. I had planned everything, but I had neglected to check my equipment. I knew that the ferrule on my flyrod was loose, but had kept putting the repair job off. To prevent anything like that happening again, each winter I check all my fishing tackle. Here's what I do.

First I check my rods. I see that all ferrules and guides are on tight. I check the guides to see if grooves are worn in them. If so, I replace them. A worn guide will cause any line to wear thin and eventually break. I also check the windings, applying clear lacquer with a camel-hair brush wherever needed.

Next, I take my reels apart, checking each part for wear. I wash the reel in a coffee can filled with turpentine. Then I apply a light coat of fine oil to the parts and reassemble the reels. The final touch is to apply a drop of clear nail polish on all screws so they can't work loose. I also discard all mono-filament lines that I used the previous summer. It costs but a couple of dollars to buy new lines; so why take a chance with a worn line? My silk, nylon, and fly lines I treat according to the manufacturer's instructions.

All my lures and flies are then attended to. I resharpen the hooks of every lure. I touch up all the rusted and worn and chipped spots on the lures. I tighten all screws, check all over to see that nothing can pull loose. The flies are also checked thoroughly, with new hackle and windings applied wherever necessary. I then store the flies in a sealed jar.

Like most fishermen, I do not find the things I do a chore. I spend my happy winter evenings spreading all my fishing gear out and getting everything in shape for another season. You can bet that the next time I sneak up on old Bucket Head, my equipment will be in excellent shape!

ANALYSIS: This is a conventional flashback approach in that the author catches our interest immediately with his use of dialogue and action. The technique is frequently used to add human interest to a how-to-do-it essay. Note that the flashback covers half the theme, perhaps a bit too long in a theme of five hundred words for the author's purpose of explaining how to keep fishing gear in shape. However, the second half of the theme does give enough information for most purposes. The theme obviously could have omitted the flashback and started immediately to discuss things to do.

The conclusion is appropriate in that it refers to the introduction and ends on a note of human interest.

If we question the use of a flashback for such a theme, we need only to consult the popular magazines devoted to hunting and fishing to find many articles developed using the same technique.

SAMPLE THEME—FLASHBACK:

A Ray of Light

She walks into a crowded room, and suddenly there is a reverent, hushed silence, an awe that few human beings can inspire. If respect can be felt, this person certainly must sense the wave of human emotion that reaches out to her. She smiles, and everyone smiles with her. She is erect, sure of herself; and everyone in the room stands taller because of her. As she walks through the room, the crowd falls back in waves. Certainly she must be a reigning Queen of some powerful country, or maybe a regal beauty of the stage or screen. She is none of these. She is Helen Keller, a blind and deaf woman.

Few people on this earth have overcome the great handicaps which Helen Keller overcame to become one of the best known and most admired women of any age. Many people have wondered just how anyone could overcome the triple handicaps of blindness, deafness, and mutism. There are probably several reasons that can account for her success in mastering these multiple tragedies.

One of the chief reasons for her success is the fact that she did not accept her lot. Instead, she had within her a power that fought vigorously against passively accepting a fate that seemingly would thwart any desires or ambitions a normal person would have. But Miss Keller is not normal—she is superior.

Her great need to express herself caused her parents to secure for her the wonderfully able Anne Sullivan, who thereafter became Helen's constant companion. The patience and wisdom of this kind woman no doubt played a great part in the success of Helen Keller. Miss Sullivan spent long, laborious hours teaching her young pupil to connect words with objects. Later on, when Helen had learned to speak not only by Braille, but also by oral speech, Miss Sullivan accompanied her on her many tours and lectures.

Another important factor in Miss Keller's success was her great determination and perseverance. She would read by Braille until her bleeding fingers had to be bandaged with silk before she could continue. This determination led her to complete college and accomplish other feats which have inspired people of all levels and of all countries.

One could go on talking about this remarkable woman. But there is no need to further praise her. Suffice it to say that for many people and for me, Miss Keller is a ray of light.

ANALYSIS: In her flashback, the author has wisely used a present tense description of Helen Keller to add a touch of immediacy and human interest to what is essentially a description of how one person overcame her handicaps. If we look closely, we can see that the author could have omitted the first paragraph and, without changing a word, used paragraph two as an introduction. Note that the first sentence of paragraph two is actually the thesis sentence. The use of a flashback in such a situation, is conventional. Many articles describing famous people's conquest of misfortune, pain, or poverty begin with a flashback.

The conclusion is conventional and is called for by the points discussed. Note that the last sentence repeats the title, a wise way to unify the theme.

SUGGESTED TOPICS FOR FLASHBACK THEMES:

1. A Day I'll Never Forget

2. A Case of Mob Action

3. Man—Nature's Worst Enemy

4. A Sportsman's Paradise

5. A Loser Becomes a Winner

6. Catch that Lunker Fish

7. Experience Pays Off

8. I Learned the Hard Way

9. There's More to Cooking than Recipes

10. Plan before Acting

HOW-TO; HOW IT IS DONE

A how-to theme implies that the writer knows how to do what he is discussing, whether it be hunting rabbits, cleaning a chicken, baking bread, or avoiding work. In such a theme the writer not only has to organize his presentation, he should also be correct in his facts. A factual error is as serious as one in grammar.

A how-it-is-done theme can be based upon personal experience or upon research. You may not be a champion swimmer, but if you have watched a champion swimmer in his months and years of practice, you could write a theme on how he became the champion. Similarly, you could be interested in how leather is tanned and do sufficient research to write a competent theme.

Whatever your topic, a step-by-step approach is mandatory. Thus, a preliminary jotting down of the details to be discussed is called for. Facts, details, do's and don't's, cautions, tips, explanations—all are needed and should be itemized before the theme is written. In short, the more care you take before actually writing your theme, the easier the writing will be.

APPLICATION: Now study the suggestions and read the list of do's and don't's. Then read each theme, including the analysis given. As you read each theme, refer to the suggestions and the list to see how the theme has implemented them. Once you have a good idea of what to do, look at the suggested list of topics and decide what your topic will be. When you have written your first draft, recheck the suggestions to see if you have included everything.

SUGGESTIONS: Most how-to themes have a prefatory paragraph which discusses the reasons why the author is writing the paper. A good opening is to ask the reader a question or two. The opening and the development of either how-to or how-it-is-done themes will be similar. Explanations, warnings, hints, do's and don'ts, etc., should come where they are needed, not at the conclusion of the theme.

Paragraphs are short. Sentences are short. Clearness and exactness are more important than literary effectiveness or strict adherence to paragraphing, topic sentences, and the like. Most how-to articles list items needed, and so on, at the end. Tell the reader at the beginning that such information is included.

Your conclusion will probably be a formula ending. That is, it will state that if "instructions are followed," the reader will meet with success.

DO'S AND DON'T'S:

1. Remember that a how-to theme demands that the author be an expert. A how-it-is-done theme in most cases will call for research.

2. Determine your audience. For instance, an article on how to make a chest of drawers would be much more detailed and explanatory if it were for novices than if it were for craftsmen.

3. Do remember that logical development is mandatory. Do not wait until the last paragraph to explain things needed as they logically come up.

4. It is best to set off tables, dimensions, and so on, rather than try to incorporate them in text.

5. In many cases, you also have to say why something is done, not merely how.

6. Do use charts, maps, pictures, illustrations, tables, and so on, which are clearly labelled. The more detailed your paper, the more such material is needed.

7. Do note the techniques used in how-to articles written in the popular magazines.

8. If you are writing a how-to theme, the same demands upon organization, knowledge, and expertness are called for.

9. Do not combine how-to papers with narration, flashbacks, and the like. The essence is clearness and exactness, not literary technique.

10. Do not attempt too big a project for theme purposes. Build a bird house, not a house.

11. Beware of "humorous" how-to themes. Student humor is frequently far short of what is imagined. Irony is not easy to master.

12. Do not forget to include the don'ts. That is, warn the reader of the pitfalls, dangers, and so forth, that he will run across.

13. Check the PROOFREADING CHART.

SAMPLE THEME—HOW TO:

Building an Organ

Two years ago, I broke my leg. I was sent home from the hospital with my leg in a cast, and I faced a long, hot summer waiting for my leg to heal. My father, knowing that I would need something to pass the time, ordered an electric organ kit for me to build. I had never worked with electronics before, but when the kit arrived and we unpacked it, I saw that I would have a fascinating time. It may appear difficult, but building an organ is a simple matter of following the detailed instruction book. Here, in brief, is how to do it.

The kit arrived in three huge boxes. One box was the wooden cabinet, already assembled. The other boxes held smaller boxes, each one numbered. The instructions said to open box number one and complete the assembly, then number two, and so on.

The foot pedal assembly was first. It involved fitting thirteen white and black pedals or keys to a steel frame. A few solders, a few nuts and bolts and tension springs, and the assembly was then ready to bolt to the bottom of the cabinet.

Next came the swell and great keyboards. Each keyboard had a total of thirty-seven keys to fit on a steel frame, much like the foot pedal assembly. There was much bolting, fitting of parts, soldering, and so on, but most of it was routine, the same thing over and over. Once both keyboards were assembled, they were put aside until needed.

I then came to the more difficult parts of the assembly. In brief, there were an amplifier, eleven tone-generator boards (the factory had already built the "C" board from which all boards were tuned), a distribution circuit board, and two other small boards which held about thirty or forty parts each. Each of these components was packed separately, each was assembled separately, and each was placed in its proper place when finally assembled. While there was much soldering, bending, wire-cutting, and so on, the detailed instructions made it easy to understand and to do. I never became bored with any of these components because none of them took long periods of time to complete. In addition, I could stop whenever I wanted to because the instruction book had little boxes to check as each part was completed.

The last major components were the two control panels. The upper panel had six "voices"; the lower had four. These panels also had the on-off switch and various other controls.

Then, the job became one of connecting all the components. The factory had furnished complete wiring and cable harnesses, and so the connecting of red wires to red wires, blue to blue, and so on, was not difficult.

The last thing to place in the organ was the speaker. Once it was bolted in place and the wires hooked on, I plugged in the electric cord, held my breath, and turned the organ on. It worked! That is, it squealed and groaned and shook, but it was alive!

The final steps were simply to resolder here, tighten there, bend something else, and then tune the organ. All this construction took me about a month. If I had not had a broken leg, I could have finished it sooner. And if my father had not "helped" me, I could have finished it in two weeks.

ANALYSIS: This is really not a how-to-do-it theme, but a discussion of how the author built an organ following a very detailed "how-to" manual. Obviously, a complete how-to discussion would have to include all the instructions found in the builder's manual—a book, not a theme. Still, the theme adequately describes the high spots of the building process and assures the reader that he, too, could construct an organ. Note that the tone of the theme also contributes to the author's intention of assuring us that the process is not too difficult.

The paragraphing, of course, is not difficult. The author merely had to follow the process he used in the construction of the organ, and the paragraphing took care of itself.

Note that the conclusion also contributes to the human interest. In a formal how-to discussion, of course, no final light touch would be needed.

SAMPLE THEME—HOW IT IS DONE:

The Big Ones

One of the favorite sayings in the magazines devoted to fishing is that "Ten per cent of the fishermen catch ninety per cent of the fish." I find nothing to argue about over these figures, for I believe that they are close to the truth. Why is this so? In the following paragraphs, I shall present my opinion on how they do it.

First of all, real fishermen fish. They are not just once-a-week fishermen. They have the time, the money, and the opportunities to fish which the average fisherman does not have. They are fishing three, four, five times a week; and they are fishing for long stretches of time. With this experience, they get to know the local waters like their kitchens. They also get to know the good and bad spots, the movement of fish, and so on.

Secondly, they have proper equipment. The old cartoon of the barefoot boy with safety-pin hook and a can of worms and a huge string of fish is strictly a "fish story." The experts have proper rods and reels, lines, lures. They also have boats, motors, boots, all kinds of equipment which enable them to spend long, pleasant days at their sport.

Thirdly, the experts fish the waters where the fish are. The typical unsuccessful fisherman spends perhaps a few hours on weekends on the banks of the local reservoir, banks worn bare by the hundreds of other unsuccessful fishermen who walk around it day after day, and with perhaps a hundred speedboats and water skiers churning the water to a soupy mess. The expert is on other waters; he's on the big TVA lakes, or in upper Canada, or in wild and remote areas. He's on the seldom-fished big waters where the big fish are. And, of course, he's there when the fish are biting, not on a hot Sunday afternoon when even the mosquitoes are waiting for the cool evening before biting. Obviously, this big-water fishing takes time and money, something that ninety per cent of fishermen do not have.

And finally, the expert has a guide. When he goes off to fish, he has the money to hire a local guide who can take him to the exact spot at the right time with the right lure. The two of them jump into a boat; the guide takes over. After a run to the fishing waters, the guide stops the boat, points, and grunts, "Old line-buster here. Put on number two wobbler, throw out fifty feet, count to ten, and strike hard." The modern guide also has a camera along to take the picture of the expert holding up "old line-buster." It is a "package deal." Many of the advertisements in the sport magazines guarantee results—no fish, no pay.

So there you have my opinion about who catches the fish and how they do it. Of course, becoming an expert fisherman has its drawbacks: it becomes more of a chore than a recreation when one attacks it as a full-time avocation.

ANALYSIS: Note that the author wisely says in his first paragraph that his discussion is "my own opinion." He could, in other words, be wrong about how big fish are caught, but his theories stand correct until disproved.

The development is DEDUCTIVE, with the thesis being how ten per cent of the fishermen catch ninety per cent of the fish. Then, paragraphs two, three, four, and five discuss in turn the author's four contentions. The discussion is quite logical, so much so that the reader has a strong feeling that the author knows what he is talking about.

Note that since we have the feeling that the author is a bit bitter, he wisely concludes his theme on the reflective note that he will take his chances as ninety per cent of the fishermen do and that he will, as a consequence, still enjoy fishing.

SUGGESTED TOPICS FOR HOW-TO AND HOW-IT-IS-DONE THEMES:

1. How to Change a Tire

2. Making a Dress

3. The Art of Being Popular

4. Getting Ahead in School

5. How to Study

6. How to Remain Single

7. How to be Expelled

8. Building a Conference Champion

9. Raising Crops

10. Teaching Your Dog to Obey

11. How to be Elected

12. Building a Tree House

13. Cake Baking Made Easy

14. How to Lose Friends

15. How to Have a Shower

16. Steel Making (needs research)

17. Tanning Leather (needs research)

18. How an Assembly Line Works (needs research)

19. How to Waterproof Material (needs research)

20. Why Graduate School Takes so Long (needs research)

IMITATIVE

In imitating an author's style, one must study his mannerisms, vocabulary, sentence structure, tone, subject matter, and so on. Those authors with a pronounced style—Hemingway, Poe, Mencken, and the like—are easily imitated, but we must remember that they were masters of their trade. Do not attempt to pattern your style after them in everything you write. It is amusing and interesting to try to write like an admired author, but an essay patterned after another's style should be attempted only as an exercise.

It is much easier to imitate a type—a fable, a parable, "twist ending" (O. Henry's device), "stream of consciousness" (James Joyce's device), and so on. Here, all one has to do is follow the technique of the model. A fable or a parable thus will have a moral, a twist ending will surprise the reader in concluding in an unexpected way, and a stream of consciousness will involve putting on paper the thoughts which flow through one's mind.

Remember that no matter what imitation you attempt, your theme should be grammatically correct, organized, logical, unified. It is still a theme to be evaluated, not a literary production to be admired.

APPLICATION: Now study the suggestions and read the list of do's and don't's. Then read each theme, including the analysis given. As you read each theme, refer to the suggestions and the list to see how the theme has implemented them. Once you have a good idea of what to do, look at the suggested list of topics and decide what your topic will be. When you have written your first draft, recheck the suggestions to see if you have included everything.

SUGGESTIONS: The development of an imitation theme will follow that of your model. Usually, imitations are of fiction and of poetry, not of expository writing. Note that rigid rules of paragraphing, called for by the rules of expository writing, are not always followed by professional writers, who paragraph more by instinct and for stylistic reasons. Do not try to have a topic sentence for each paragraph unless your model has one.

Note that conclusions are not tidy "wrap-ups." Professional writers avoid formula endings. Their endings fit their style.

DO'S AND DON'T'S:

1. Check with your teacher before writing an imitation or a parody of the work of a professional.

2. Remember that imitating another does not justify your making mistakes in the mechanics.

3. Most imitations take the form of a parody. If you are a novice writer, it is best to stick to those authors whose style is quite obvious: Poe, Hemingway, James, Twain, and the like.

4. Also remember that clever parodies have probably also been done before by other students. In short, do not expect that your cleverness will astound your reader.

5. "Slanting" is imitative. A slanted article is one written after you study the publication you wish to accept your work. You follow the rules, length, style, type of writing, etc., of the publication you are interested in.

6. Don't assume that vocabulary is sufficient to produce an imitation. Sentence length; the rhythm, variety, and kinds of sentences; verbs, adjectives, placement of modifiers; figures of speech, tone, mood, subject matter—a host of things determine an author's style.

7. Don't try to mold your own style to another's style. It is good for beginning writers to admire and study the work of a professional, but slavish imitation is never the route to developing your own individual approach.

8. If you cannot imitate another's style of writing, you could try to imitate a type of writing or speaking—fable, a sermon, a sales "pitch," a carnival barker, or a tour guide's memorized speech. Ordinarily, in this type of writing, you will state in your first paragraph what you are doing.

9. Check the PROOFREADING CHART.

SAMPLE THEME—IMITATIVE OF EDGAR ALLAN POE:

Naomi

I find myself recalling the vision of a girl I knew in the seemingly roseate days of my youth. I think of her so often that at times the thoughts are as joys unknown; and then again, the thoughts I have of her are tinged with melancholy.

She was Naomi. I recall her now as a dream shimmering faintly upon the lake of pleasant reveries. I seem to sense her hand reach out for me and to hear her voice call out to me through the mists that cloud the years. Faintly and hauntingly, the call beats through my mind as if it were a drum of some jungle madness. Naomi! Naomi! Naomi!

She was the breath of life, the song of summer nights, the

sob of winds, and the pain of lost love to me. She was my seasons; she was my years. She was all that was all to me; she was all that was not for me.

She was a long journey. She was like going home. She was like leaving home forever. She was nights spent in dreaming and days spent in doing. She was a word, a thought, a cry, a laugh, a walk through green fields, a wind-blown, tree-topped hill.

She was music dancing on flowers and love playing blindman's-buff with fate. She was all that mattered to me. She was all that I wished for and all that I longed for.

Then one day she stole away from me as a wraith at twilight, softly, with no word save a laugh echoing mockingly on the vibrant air.

Now she is gone forever. Nothing remains but the heart of me, a memory that will not die until at last the blessed sleep descends.

ANALYSIS: This theme succeeds not so much because it is an accurate imitation of Poe's style, but because in comparison with the usual theme on a conventional topic which the instructor must read, it is a different, fresh, "literary" theme. To be sure, some of the elements of Poe's style are present: word choice, tone, mood, figures of speech. And the theme of the loss of a loved one is, of course, one of Poe's favorite topics.

Note that the paragraphing is not based upon the use of topic sentences, nor does it follow Poe's style. Rather, each paragraph is a grouping of images into short, manageable length. The short paragraphs give us an opportunity to pause before continuing to read what is essentially a long series of figures of speech—much the same pause that we make in reading stanzas in poetry.

SAMPLE THEME—IMITATIVE OF A TYPE:

A Fable of Moderns, or How Geometry Got One of Its Rules

Once upon a time there lived an exceedingly brave and handsome Indian warrior. Not only did he govern his tribe well,
but he also was an excellent leader on the field of battle.
Accordingly, he was frequently away fighting.

It so happened that while he was away on a particularly long
excursion, his three wives all had babies. In a manner which
would be fitting for so great a warrior, the three wives decided
to do something special for the chief when he arrived home.

At length, news came back that the successful band of warriors was approaching. The three wives stirred themselves,
put on their best attire, and each displayed her offspring on an
animal outside the tepee. The first wife placed her baby on a
buffalo hide. The second wife placed her baby on a horse
hide. The third wife, since she had twins, decided that something more ornate was called for, and so she placed her
twins on a hippopotamus hide.

Soon the band of warriors arrived. The handsome and brave
chief was last to enter the village. As was his custom, he did
not talk, did not show any display of emotion. He let the
lesser warriors do the bragging and the telling of their heroic
exploits. The three wives, knowing their husband well, pa-
tiently sat on the hides, their babies at their side, on display
for their lord and master.

The chief walked slowly along the line of hides. He looked
at the first baby and grunted. He looked at the second baby
and grunted. The third hide, however, with its twins, caused
him to pause. Slowly, his eyes moved from baby to baby. At
length he turned to his assistants and commented: "Ugh! The
sons of the squaw of the hippopotamus are equal to the sons
of the squaws of the two hides."

ANALYSIS: This imitation of a type is much easier to write
than is the imitation of a style that we find in the previous
theme. In short, imitating a kind or type of prose is not so
much an imitation as it is a form of development.

As a fable, the theme succeeds: it uses the conventional intro-
duction-story-moral method that we expect in a fable; and the

theme also succeeds because of the novelty (perhaps a bit strained) of the fable told. Obviously, the author did not write an original fable, but one of the elements of a fable is the implication that it is a retelling of a story. The success of this theme, of course, depends upon our willingness to accept the "punch line." Whether we do or not, however, the student has written a good fable.

SUGGESTED IMITATIVE TOPICS AND STYLES:

1. Poe's use of mood and tone

2. Hemingway's terse style

3. Franklin's "almanac" style

4. "Purple prose"

5. "Stream of consciousness" style of Woolf or Joyce

6. The style of *Time* magazine

7. Browning's dramatic monologs

8. Francis Bacon's compact essay style

9. Edgar Lee Master's soliloquy style

10. H. L. Mencken's invective style

IMPLIED

Since teachers of composition are quite firm in their insistance that themes be organized with a definite thesis sentence and with each paragraph having a topic sentence, a theme with an implied thesis should be avoided unless you first check with your teacher.

The dangers of using an implied thesis are that the reader may get an entirely different implication from that intended, or that two or more implications can easily be drawn from the reading, or that no implication at all can be drawn. One of the major errors made by young writers is that of lack of focus; a series of sentences may ramble on without saying anything in particular or without arriving at a logical conclusion. Unless your implication is very obvious, do not write such a theme. If you decide to write such a theme, read it to a fellow student and ask him what the thesis is. If he does not immediately know, rewrite the theme using a stated thesis.

APPLICATION: Now study the suggestions and read the list of do's and don't's. Then read each theme, including the analysis given. As you read each theme, refer to the suggestions and the list to see how the theme has implemented them. Once you have a good idea of what to do, look at the suggested list of topics and decide what your topic will be. When you have written your first draft, recheck the suggestions to see if you have included everything.

SUGGESTIONS: Since the generalization you are writing about is not stated in an implied theme, your development begins immediately. Each paragraph will be another point which should inescapably lead the reader to come to the same conclusion you have in mind.

Each paragraph should "build your case" without so stating. Do not weakly hint what your generalization is. Either state it, (DEDUCTIVE form), or make sure that your thesis is obviously apparent. Ending each paragraph with a question for the reader to answer is a very good way to make your implication stronger.

At the end of the theme the reader is left to draw his own conclusion. End with a question, such as "When are we going to wake up?" or "What are we going to do about this?"

DO'S AND DON'T'S:

1. For novice writers, implied generalizations are dangerous. Unless you know what you are about, it is better to use a form where you definitely state your thesis.

2. Use many questions, but let the reader formulate his own answer. End each paragraph with a question.

3. Implied writings are frequently ironical pieces. The danger of using irony is twofold: you may not make irony clear; and, no matter how clear, many readers never "get the point" and thus the irony has the opposite effect from what you intended.

4. Note that many "low-key" advertisements make their point, not by telling you to buy, but by so describing the value, merit, enjoyment, and security of the product that the implication about which product you should buy is obvious. Thus word choice and tone are extremely important in this kind of writing.

5. Do not write a theme with an implied moral, point, or subject, unless your teacher is first consulted.

6. Be sure that the implication which seems obvious to you will also be obvious to your reader.

7. Consider using either the DEDUCTIVE of the INDUCTIVE FORM. Is your intended implied approach better?

8. Do not "give your plot away" in the title.

9. Check the PROOFREADING CHART.

SAMPLE THEME—IMPLIED THESIS: The student who wrote the following theme had an implied thesis in mind. Does the reader immediately grasp the implication, or is there another implication?

My Teachers

Miss Ripley, my biology teacher, does not know that students exist. She comes to class late, keeps us after the bell, forgets to make assignments, and then covers half the book in one week. She announced that we would have a weekly test, but so far we have had short tests practically every class.

Mr. Rogers, my history teacher, is what I would call a grouch. He yells at the class. He likes to give "pop" tests. He makes all the girls sit in the back of the room. If anyone slouches, he makes him sit up. If we do not bring our books to class, he makes us go get them. Most of us feel that he would make a better drill sergeant than a teacher.

Mr. Bronson is the opposite of Mr. Rogers. He smiles all the time. He tries so hard to be popular that all the poor students try to get in his class. His tests are too easy, and he doesn't test us on anything that he does not discuss in class. As a result, most of us feel that we are getting three hours' credit for doing nothing.

Mr. Leggett, my physical education teacher, probably came down from the trees to teach. I have never seen him without sweat clothes on, and so I don't know if he ever wore a tie or not. He teaches his classes as though we were preparing for the Olympics. We don't have to worry about his grades, though, because the rumor on campus is that he knows only how to write A, B, and C.

So, if I had to vote on which of my teachers is the worst, I really couldn't decide. It would be like trying to pick out the worst peanut in a truckload of them.

ANALYSIS: As suggested in the note preceding the theme, the student's implication is ambiguous. The concluding paragraph, of course, all but states the thesis intended: "My teachers are bad." Some readers may accept it. But some readers could just as easily supply another thesis: "This student is a bad whiner."

Aside from the ambiguity of the thesis, the student comes close to the purpose. He would have a better theme had he not been so bitter, had he written his paper on a lighter note, and had he used a touch of charity in his discussion so that we could read a fair description of his teachers and then make up our own minds.

The theme, for many readers, then, fails because the author tries too hard to make his implication clear. The theme as it stands would be better if developed with a stated thesis, either in the beginning (DEDUCTIVE) or at the end (INDUCTIVE).

SAMPLE THEME—IMPLIED THESIS:

The Truly Famous Belchfire Six, Eight, and Twelve

Belchfire Automobiles announces its new line of Belchfire Sixes, Eights, and Twelves for the coming year.

Wise buyers have a choice of three engines, famous in the industry, with horsepower ranging between 20 to 100 in the Six, 85 to 220 in the Eight, and 250 to 500 in the Twelve. Each of these engines is available in our Wun-dor, Two-dor, Four-dor, Nodor, sedan, hardtop, ragtop, No-top, Flip-top, Tip-top models. A wide choice of colors is available, ranging from the popular six shades of white through the traditional eighteen shades of off-black. In all, 18,358 color combinations are available. Luxurious matching interiors, famous in the Industry, ranging from basic burlap to imported Formalde Hide, are available.

The Belchfire accessories, famous in the field, include those tried-and-true features which have proved so popular in the past. Included on the new models are such optional extras as running boards, radiator thermometer, 2, 3, 4, 5, or 6 on the floor, dual controls, matched luggage and jack, helium filled tires, shower stall, and a drinking fountain.

Gas and oil, water for the radiator and the window washers, air for the tires—each molecule is severely limited by the famous Belchfire Gag System, unequalled by the other luxury cars.

Speed, power, and fast getaways are entirely sufficient, befitting the look of galvanized energy famous in the Industry.

Belchfire Automobiles, famous in the Industry, wishes to remind you that a man driving a Belchfire is a man on the move!

ANALYSIS: This theme is of course a satire and succeeds, if we accept it as such, with the implied thesis being something like "Automobile advertisements are ridiculous." (Satire makes use of wit, irony, or sarcasm to expose or discredit vice or folly.) But since we are amused by the author's clever repetition, his wide-ranging imagination, and his good parody in the concluding paragraph, we enjoy the theme without needing to state accurately what the thesis is.

There is danger, however, in satire. Some readers will not "get the point" of any satire, no matter how broad, and will draw entirely different conclusions about the writing, the thesis, and the author. No matter how obvious a satire may be, there are sure to be some who are not amused. This is particularly true in the case of those at whom the satire is directed.

For a young writer, it is often difficult to write satire in which the intent is serious. At the beginning the student may feel more comfortable dealing with satire which is not meant to change things, or to argue a point—that is, satire which is used only to amuse.

SUGGESTED TOPICS FOR IMPLIED THEMES:

1. Should America "Turn the Other Cheek?"

2. Our Polluted Waters

3. Strip Mining Havoc

4. The School Paper—Spokesman for Whom?

5. Gun Laws

6. Are We Mice or Men?

7. And They Call It a "Cold War!"

8. "It's for your own good."

9. Buy Now, Pay Forever

10. This is Culture?

11. Who Owns Us?

12. My Country, Right or Wrong?

13. This is Teaching?

14. This is Living?

15. These Are Authorities?

INDUCTIVE

The inductive form of development is just the opposite of the deductive form (turn to the DEDUCTIVE section and read the introductory remarks). In the inductive form, you save the generalization for the end. A child who says "Because you're mean and nasty, I don't like you!" is using an inductive form: the particulars "mean and nasty" lead to the generalization, "I don't like you!" Any group of statements which leads to a generalization which can be made about them is in essence an inductive development.

Practically any deductive theme can be made into an inductive one. For instance, turn to the discussion 'TO THE STUDENT' at the front of this book. Note that the deductive theme presented there could easily be made inductive by omitting the generalization in the first paragraph— "My three guns are all I need to hunt in this area."—and by placing it in the final paragraph.

If you are in doubt about "saving for the end" any generalization you might make, note in the list of Do's and Don't's the kinds of topics for which the form is best suited.

APPLICATION: Now study the suggestions and read the list of do's and don't's. Then read each theme, including the analysis given. As you read each theme, refer to the suggestions and the list to see how the theme has implemented them. Once you have a good idea of what to-do, look at the suggested list of topics and decide what your topic will be. When you have written your first draft, recheck the suggestions to see if you have included everything.

SUGGESTIONS: Do not state the thesis of an inductive theme or "give the plot away" until your last paragraph. If you must, then see DEDUCTIVE form. You can hint, suggest that the conclusion will be different, amusing, or the like, if the facts or points you are to present so justify. Your introduction, however, must be valid, not just a series of idle remarks.

Each particular will probably have a separate paragraph, though it is possible to discuss more than one particular in any one paragraph, or to discuss a particular in more than one paragraph. Arrange your particulars in a logical order: chronological, ascending importance, and so on. It is the usual practice to save the most important point for the next-to-last-paragraph position.

The conclusion, generalization, or thesis is stated in the final paragraph. The above points should inescapably lead to this conclusion. See also DEDUCTIVE and IMPLIED sections.

DO'S AND DON'T'S:

1. Check to see if the DEDUCTIVE form would not be a better presentation.

2. Make sure the points presented justify the conclusion you come to.

3. Remember that inductive writing usually gives only probability, not certainty.

4. Check words like *always, all, everyone*. It is usually better to use qualifying words. See DEFINITIONS. See also "Title" on PROOFREADING CHART.

5. Save the topic sentence until the end.

6. The inductive form is used for fables, parables, proclamations, edicts, detective stories, morals, generalizations, scientific reports, and the like. Any paper which presents a series of points and concludes with words like *therefore, thus, and so,* and the like, is an inductive form.

7. Remember that the inductive form is "scientific"—reason-

ing which, by observing something to be true in numerous similar circumstances, thus concludes that it will be true in all similar circumstances.

8. Define any terms which will clarify your meaning.

9. Arrange your points in increasing (ascending) order of importance, proof, weight, etc.

10. Do not ignore exceptions or facts which an opponent would point out.

11. Do not take for granted that everyone will agree with your particulars. You need facts, figures, charts, authorities, and so on, to back your points.

12. Remember that since inductive generalizations are not determined in advance, they are made only when the accumulated evidence justifies them.

13. Do not use analogies as proof. Analogies are rhetorical devices to clarify, not justify. See ANALOGY section.

14. Check the PROOFREADING CHART.

SAMPLE THEME—INDUCTIVE:

Fisherman's Paradise

Arising at four and working on an outboard motor for thirty minutes put the fisherman over the hatching flies at approximately the right time. As the tiny winged insects rise to the surface for their flight into the woods which surrounds the lake, the water becomes alive with the rising insects and the flurry of the scrappy bream which are enjoying a once-a-year feast. The fisherman, equipped with a fly rod and white popping bugs, has roughly three hours of fishing each morning; this is so fast that there is not time to smoke, much less to string his catch. Fishermen come each year from as far away as Canada to enjoy the four to six weeks of unexcelled bream fishing on the lake.

When the flies have quit surfacing and the shallow water is once again quiet because the bream have stopped surface feeding, the fisherman simply moves to water which is deeper where he drifts with the current, fishing deep with minnows until he gets his first bite. As soon as he gets a bite, he anchors the boat and begins to haul the black and white slab crappies into the boat. Few places in the world offer so many crappies in so short a time. Several years ago, when the creel limit was forty, it was not uncommon for a boat to return to the dock in two hours with limits for everyone in the boat. These crappies bite all through the heat of the day, and only slow down in the late afternoon when they move to shallow water in search of minnows and insects.

By late afternoon, the fisherman has moved to the shallow water "jumps" and is carefully spinning his silver spoon into the brush and stumps which shelter the largemouthed bass. This torpedo of the lake sometimes reaches a weight of from twelve to fifteen pounds and is always savagely hungry in the late afternoon. It slashes through a school of shad and then comes back to pick up the dead and crippled minnows. At this time, any kind of silver spoon or spinner will result in a strike. This warfare between shad and bass, and between man and bass, will last into the darkness.

With from four to six weeks of guaranteed fishing like this each summer, fishermen make reservations at the resorts well in advance, frequently for years ahead. Most of the lake resorts are filled for the summer by the preceding Easter of each year. It is no wonder that Kentucky Lake is called by fishermen all over the country "The Fisherman's Paradise of the South."

ANALYSIS: This is an excellent inductive development. The author skillfully whets our appetite by detailed descriptions of the kinds of fishing available. Paragraph by paragraph he piles up details, perhaps using a bit of fishermen's exaggeration, until only a totally uninterested person does not wish to "peek at the ending" to see where this paradise is located. In short, all the particulars lead to the generalization that Kentucky Lake is the paradise being discussed.

This inductive development, in short, builds to a climax just as a well-written story does. The author could have used the DEDUCTIVE or the CLASSIC development, but the heightened interest he gains by withholding the generalization adds considerably to the effectiveness of the theme.

SAMPLE THEME—INDUCTIVE:

If at First You Don't Succeed, Give up!

The main points of this theme were separate news items written for our school paper, but since none appeared in the paper, I feel justified in using them for this class theme. The story behind them? It's the old lament which occurs on many colleges campuses.

If you will look at our school paper, you will note that on the masthead it states, "Written by the students for the good of the school." I'll reserve comment until I present my case.

Item one: I wrote an editorial saying that the Council was nothing but a rubber stamp for the Administration. Why else would the Council pass a resolution banning cars for undergraduates, unless pressure was put on the Council? So with the "approval" of the Council, the Administration has barred cars for freshmen. The following year, it will be the sophomores. I knew my editorial would not be printed, but I wrote it to let off steam.

Item two: We had a "Most Popular Teacher" campaign a few weeks ago. Students dropped their ballots off at the Union, and many did vote. Who won? We'll never know. The ballots were "misplaced," or so we were told. What really happened, and why hasn't the paper mentioned the contest?

Item three: It is known all over campus that last year a few of our "all Americans" broke into one of the offices and stole copies of an examination. It is also known that their penalty consisted of being barred from attending summer school. Horrors! Is our conference championship worth all this? Why was the editorial discussing the case not printed?

My comments are really not needed, but I would like to make

one suggestion: let's change the motto from "Written by students for the good of the school" to something more appropriate, say "All the news the Administration thinks you should have."

ANALYSIS: This inductive approach is passable, but it is not so successful as that in the previous theme. True, the author gives us some particulars and probably is satisfied that his generalization is valid: the school paper is nothing but a mouthpiece for the administration. The questions we must ask are whether the details are sufficient and whether another development—DEDUCTIVE or CLASSIC—might not have been better. Note that the author does skillfully introduce his discussion by stating that he will first present his case before making a judgment.

We must agree that the author does have an inductive development and that he has some valid particulars. An insertion of a qualifying word like "perhaps," or a qualifying phrase like "it seems to me" in his generalization might not have been a bad idea; doesn't "It seems to me that our paper prints all the news the Administration thinks you should have" leave the author on safer ground?

SUGGESTED TOPICS FOR INDUCTIVE THEMES:

1. A Truth I Learned

2. The Person I Married

3. A Student's Proclamation

4. A Modern Fable

5. Automobile Insurance

6. Lose a Friend

7. How to Learn the Hard Way

8. Experience Teaches a Dear School

9. The Best Bargain

10. "And so I Say to You. . ."

11. A New Truth?

12. Who Killed Our Morale?

13. A Student Manifesto

14. I Should Have Listened

15. Three Becauses in Search of a Therefore

SPACE FILLER

The term "space filler" has been applied to this section as a deliberate warning to the student writing without a definitely stated thesis. (See also the IMPLIED section.) The term is perhaps unfair, because many famous writers have written and are writing daily, weekly, or monthly columns of a space-filler nature which are highly respected and read by millions. The columns can be found in all the better newspapers and magazines.

However, since you are taking a course where expository writing is expected, you should remember that exposition means an organized, logical, unified, coherent setting forth of a thesis which expounds, explains, or appraises analytically. In short, your theme should talk about one thing, and each and every paragraph in the theme should be directly and unmistakably related to that one thing.

If you insist, however, that you have three or four interesting items for a theme, then relate them to each other. If they are amusing, interesting, a commentary upon the times, or the like, devise a thesis which states the area the items will cover and write the theme using one of the standard forms of development—perhaps INDUCTIVE, DEDUCTIVE, COMPARE AND CONTRAST, or CLASSIFICATION.

APPLICATION: Now study the suggestions and read the list of do's and don't's. Then read each theme, including the analysis given. As you read each theme, refer to the suggestions and the list to see how the theme has implemented them. Once you see how easy it is to have a thesis sentence, you will not make the mistake of stringing an unrelated group of paragraphs together.

SUGGESTIONS: The introduction states or implies that what follows is a miscellaneous "clean up the desk" collection. The tone is light, half apologetic. Frequently such essays are printed with double spacing between items, or some sort of printer's mark between items to signify that they are not related. If the items are related, judicious use of transitions and topic sentences could readily make the selections into a theme.

There is no particular order of presentation. The most important or interesting could come first, in the middle or last. Present the items in the order which seems most logical, if they are related to one another in any logical way. For example, item two may or may not be related to the above or following topics. Conclusions vary widely. There may be none. It may be a half-hearted apology. Space limitations usually dictate the kind and extent of concluding remarks.

DO'S AND DON'T'S:

1. Do not write this type of paper unless you have first checked with your teacher. It is appropriate for human-interest and sports columns found in magazines and newspapers. It is not appropriate for purposes of developing skills in organizing class themes, nor is it appropriate for essay examinations.

2. Usually space fillers do have a controlling idea, perhaps one of humorous signs seen while driving, or one dealing with typographical errors, and the like. As such, they are following the DEDUCTIVE form. Such a development is acceptable for themes if the thesis is stated and if judicious use of transitions ties the ideas together.

3. When written by professionals, space fillers are interesting and may have many regular readers, many of whom con-

tribute material to the authors. The form, however, is best reserved for professionals.

4. Note how the illustrative space filler could easily be made into an acceptable theme by having a thesis sentence in the first paragraph and by introducing each series of particulars in a regular paragraph fashion.

5. Check the PROOFREADING CHART.

SAMPLE THEME—SPACE FILLER:

Those Words Again

So many letters have come in regarding our discussion in the last issue that we thought we would print some of the more interesting ones.

* * *

Mrs. L. D. Smith of Peoria asks how many of our readers could pronounce the following words correctly: impious, worsted, err, diaper, threepenny, Cairo, Illinois (both words!), Percy Bysshe Shelley, and Cholmondeley (tricky!).

* * *

Roger Jones of Chicago asks which of the following words are spelled correctly: supercede, harrass, repellant, embarass, picnicking, exagerrate, accomodate, sacreligious, seperate (watch it, proofreader!).

* * *

Bill MacAdams of Gary writes in to say that Macadamized comes from four languages: Mac from Gaelic, dam from Hebrew, iz from French, and ed from English.

* * *

Mary Burns of Toledo comments that to call a man a pagan, heathen, and barbarian really means that he lives in the provinces on a heath and wears a beard.

* * *

And finally, we do not apologize for the following puns. We think that they are the best of a lot of really bad ones. Barney Rich (no address) writes to ask if we have heard about the midget who escaped from Czechoslovakia and roamed about in Europe asking if anyone could cache a small Czech. Ernest Caldwell of Tulsa writes to tell us of a rancher who left his ranch to his sons and named it Focus because it is where the sons raise meet (Ugh!). And Dick Crane of Detroit tells us that the local police threatened to close a burlesque theater because of the suggestive advertising, and so the management put up a new sign: "Hear the Belles Peel."

*   *   *

Should we continue next week, or have our readers had enough?

ANALYSIS: This is a typical collection of items for a space-filler column in a newspaper or a magazine. Because space available frequently varies from issue to issue, the writer of a space-filler column is forced to use short unrelated items or a series of unrelated items so that one or two can be left out without destroying the continuity of the article. Note that any of the items in this selection could be omitted without harm. If it were the usual thesis-and-topic-sentence, of course, omission of one or more paragraphs could leave either a confused topic or an insufficiently developed topic.

SUMMARY

In most cases, a summary is assigned so that the student can gain experience in selecting and presenting essential information found in a piece of writing. The student, of course, does this constantly in his studying and note taking. Also in library assignments, term papers, and under the pressure of time, the student frequently must condense pages of information for transfer to note cards or into his own personal notes. Obviously, to be of value, the condensation must accurately reflect the meaning of the original.

In most cases, your teacher will give instruction as to the kind and length of summary he wants. If not, remember that writers follow the same procedure in writing that you do: they use a thesis sentence, they use topic sentences in their paragraphing, they frequently repeat key ideas, they themselves summarize what they have said, usually at the end of paragraphs, sections, or the article. In short, the writing to be summarized will have a line of development with which you are familiar. Seek out these key ideas and write them down. Then, reread the selection to see if you have accurately captured the intent, purpose, and meaning of the original. You frequently may use the author's own words, or you may write his ideas in your own words.

Do not try to duplicate the paragraphing of the original. Instead, break down the information into easily managed units. Keep like ideas together, and the paragraphing will take care of itself.

You are, of course, expected to be grammatically correct. Accordingly, be sure to check the PROOFREADING CHART found in the Appendix of this book.

SUGGESTIONS: The development of a summary theme follows that of the source. If you do a thorough job, your paragraphing will take care of itself. Ordinarily, closely related ideas will be in one paragraph. Then, when the source changes to another major topic, you also can start a new paragraph.

It is not necessary to devote one paragraph to one idea. Depending upon the length of your source, one paragraph may well summarize two, three, or even dozens of paragraphs or pages of your source. Since you will have many ideas in brief form, short paragraphs will be easier to handle (and read later on) than long ones. In a summary, you do not add your own conclusion. When you have finished summarizing your source, stop.

DO'S AND DON'T'S:

1. Remember that the purpose of a summary is to select the main points from long selections. A summary is a brief presentation of the material of longer papers, essays, chapters, books, and the like.

2. Summaries vary widely. Check with your teacher for further specific suggestions if the do's and don'ts in this list seem to be too detailed.

3. Keep in mind that a summary of theme length will be

of an original that is probably at least three or four times longer. The longer the writing which is summarized, the less proportion you will give each point.

4. Thus, depending upon your purpose or your assignment, a summary of a novel could be a sentence or two, a paragraph, a theme, or a paper which is pages in length.

5. Do not summarize paragraph for paragraph. Perhaps as many as a dozen paragraphs of the original could be stated in one paragraph.

6. In general, give as much proportion in your summary as your original gives. A long illustration of a single point, of course, does not need proportionate space in your summary.

7. Read all of the original before deciding your approach. You will thus gain an idea of how much proportion each point will have.

8. The book you are now reading is a summary, a shortened form of the information to be found in books many hundreds of pages in length.

9. Don't paraphrase unless directed to. A paraphrase is a statement in your own words of what another has said. A paraphrase will be almost as long as the original.

10. Unless directed to, don't use your own interpretation, mood, opinion. Keep the meaning, intention, stress, and importance that you find in your source.

11. Avoid saying "The author says." A summary implies that someone else says it.

12. Don't slavishly use the author's words. You may select a word or phrase from the original, but in general do not quote extensively.

13. Don't misinterpret the original in your effort to be concise. Also do not omit minor points which must be con-

sidered in relation to the major points. This generalization is particularly valid if you are to put the summary aside for weeks or months before using it again.

14. Many of the points given above are for summaries which are to be handed to the teacher. For your own purposes, a summary which has the main points of the original stated clearly and logically is all that is demanded.

15. Check the PROOFREADING CHART.

SAMPLE THEME—SUMMARY:

A Summary of the Rules for Comma Usage

When main clauses are joined by the coordinating conjunctions (and, but, for, or, nor), use a comma. The three exceptions are these: 1) When the main clauses are short, a comma is not needed. Example: It was raining but I don't mind. 2) When the subject remains the same, no comma is needed. Example: I walked across the campus last night and I noticed that the lights were out. 3) When the main clauses have internal punctuation, separate the main clauses by a semicolon. Example: I noticed her dress, of course, but did not say anything; and I also noticed her jewelry, about which I had plenty to say.

When a long phrase or an adverb clause preceeds the main clause, follow it with a comma. If you will notice this sentence and the preceding one, you will see the rule illustrated. An exception is made to this rule when the introductory phrase or clause is short. Example: When it rains I stay home.

Items in series are separated by commas. Examples: I was tired, cold, and hungry. He ran into the house, down the stairs, and into the coal bin. He said that he was leaving, that he did not care what she did, and that he would never call again. Red, white, and blue are the colors of our flag.

Miscellaneous uses of the comma include the following examples: You, Bill Brown, are lazy (direct address). Bill Brown, who is lazy, will not be elected (adjective clauses—

nonrestrictive). Bill, our captain, was told to leave the game (nouns in apposition). He lives at 17 Oak Lane, Chicago, Illinois (addresses). On May 17, 1929, he was found dead (dates). You are, on the whole, a good student (parenthetical phrase). Seeing that he was cold, I fed him warm soup (participal Phrase).

Use a comma when it will prevent misreading. Examples: He cried, for his mother had left. Outside, the house was cheerful looking.

ANALYSIS: This selection adequately summarizes the traditional rules for commas. It has the brief versions of the rules and also wisely gives examples for both the rules and the exceptions. Note that a further reduction could be made by merely using the first sentence of each of the five paragraphs.

The paragraphing, of course, is simply taken care of by using one rule per paragraph. Note that neither an introduction nor a conclusion is needed.

If you wish to compare this summary with a full discussion of comma rules, consult any of the handbooks listed in the Bibliography at the end of this book.

SAMPLE THEME—SUMMARY:

A Summary of Edgar Allan Poe's "The Cask of Amontillado"

Fortunato had injured me often, but when he insulted me I vowed revenge. I did not threaten him but continued to smile in his face. He had one weakness—connoisseurship in wine —and this weakness I would use for my revenge. So, during the carnival season I arranged to meet Fortunato when he was dressed in carnival clothing and nearly drunk with celebrating. I told him that I had bought a cask of Amontillado, but that I wanted an expert like Fortunato or Luchesi to come and taste it to see if I had gotten Amontillado or a cheap substitute. Fortunato, of course, fancied himself an authority and considered Luchesi a fraud; so I knew I had him. I also protested that it was carnival time, that Fortunato was enjoying himself, that the vaults where the wine was stored were cold and damp; but by playing on his vanity, I got him to accompany me.

My palazzo I knew was empty, for I had ordered my servants not to leave; but being servants, they had fled as soon as my back was turned. I got down two flambeaux and gave one to Fortunato. We proceeded to the vaults down long, winding stairs, and finally reached the catacombs of my ancestors, the Montresors, which were below my palazzo. I warned Fortunato to be careful and suggested to him that we go no farther because his cough grew worse in the dampness, and that since he was such an important man, his death would be a blow. This play on his vanity only insured his following me. I broke off the neck of a bottle of wine and gave it to him to allay his cough, knowing that it would further intoxicate him. We drank to the bodies reposing in the catacombs.

Farther and farther we went, past many bones, casks, and finally directly beneath the river where the moisture was trickling down the walls. Again I suggested that we turn back, again he refused, again we drank another bottle of wine. He then made a motion that I did not understand. It turned out that it was a secret gesture used by the society of Freemasons. When Fortunato doubted that I was a member, I withdrew a trowel from beneath my cloak as proof—the significance and the irony of the trowel was lost on him.

Deeper went we into the vaults, finally arriving at a deep crypt. The damp, foul air caused our flambeaux to flicker. Bones were everywhere, even piled high along three walls. The fourth wall had been cleared of bones to reveal a recess four feet deep, three wide, and six or seven high. It was so dark in the recess that we could not see in. I tempted Fortunato by saying that the cask of wine was in the recess, but that perhaps Luchesi . . . Fortunato called Luchesi an ignoramus and stepped into the recess. I followed him, and before he could recover his wits, I had secured him about the waist with a lock and chain which I then fastened to two staples secured in the wall.

Now that he was mine, I played with him. I suggested that since he didn't want to return to the streets, I must then leave him. He demanded to see the wine, but I produced a quantity of stones and mortar and began to wall up the entrance. Fortunato sobered very quickly. He moaned, shook the chain. I paused to enjoy his terror. When I had bricked in the wall about halfway, I paused to look at him. He screamed, and for a moment I determined to leap in and stab him. Instead, I restrained myself and joined in with his screams as I continued my work. Finally, but one stone remained. Fortunato gave a low laugh, a laugh which made my hair stand on end. He laughed again, said it was a good joke I was playing on him, that all would laugh when they heard of it, and then suggested we return to the street. "Yes," I said, "let us be gone." "For the love of God, Montressor!" he answered. "Yes," I said, "for the love of God!" He did not reply. Twice I called his name, but all I could hear was the jingling of the chains. My heart grew sick because of the dampness, and so I hurried to force the last stone into place and plaster it. Then I pushed the bones against it. For a half century, no mortal has disturbed the bones. May Fortunato rest in peace!

ANALYSIS: This is a rather lengthy summary of the original story because the author wishes to include most of Poe's details. The summary could easily be cut in half, or a summary of one short paragraph would serve to refresh one's memory. The length of the summary depends upon the usage the student wishes to put it to.

The paragraphing does not follow the original, but is essentially a matter of breaking up the original story into five sections. The student could have used perhaps eight, nine, or ten paragraphs. Since stories are not written like a theme— stories do not use a topic sentence per paragraph—it is up to the one doing the summarizing to break up his theme into convenient sections.

Note that the student does not add his personal comments in the summary. For his own use, of course, any personal comments would add to the value of the summary when he came to use it later on.

SUGGESTED ITEMS TO SUMMARIZE: Ordinarily your teacher

will assign a selection to be summarized. If not, then any of the following would be good practice:

1. A selection in your reader, preferably an essay

2. A chapter or section of a textbook

3. An article in a magazine

4. An editorial in a newspaper

5. A television or stage play

6. A movie

7. The main plots of a novel

8. The main points of a how-to article

9. The steps to follow in building something

10. The chronology of a trip or expedition

APPENDIX

A TYPICAL GRADE SHEET

A: The *A* theme shows originality of statement and observation. Its ideas are clear, logical, and even thought provoking. It contains all the positive qualities of good writing listed below:

    1. Careful construction and organization of sentences and paragraphs.

    2. Careful choice of effective words and phrases.

    3. Adequate development of idea, or inclusion of necessary details.

    4. Absence of mechanical errors.

B: The *B* theme is logically and adequately developed. Its ideas are developed clearly because it contains some of the positive qualities of good writing. It is comparatively free of errors in the use of English. Although indicating competence, the *B* paper lacks the originality of thought and style which characterizes the *A* theme.

C: The average theme will receive a grade of *C*. It is fairly well organized and manages to convey its purpose to the reader. It avoids serious errors in the use of English. It may, in fact, have few corrections marked on it; but it lacks the vigor of thought and expression which would entitle it to a better grade.

D: The grade of *D* indicates below average achievement in expression and effectiveness. Most *D* themes contain serious errors in the use of English and fail to convey adequately the purpose of the paper. With more careful proofreading and better development, many *D* themes could be worth at least a *C* rating.

F: A grade of *F* indicates the failure to avoid serious errors in spelling, grammar, punctuation, and sentence structure. No matter how excellent the content of the paper may be, the grade of *F* will be assigned if too many gross errors appear.

HOW TO BEGIN A THEME

A good first paragraph seems very difficult. A good first sentence seems almost beyond an inexperienced writer's creative powers. What years of time are wasted by high school and college students just trying to get started! But just as there are ways of planning a paper there are also ways of planning an effective beginning.

Remember that the purpose of an introductory paragraph is to catch the reader's attention in any one of a variety of ways. While doing so, the writer must try to give a kind of capsule outline of what he is going to do in his theme. This outline will depend entirely upon what type of theme he is writing: summary, inductive, flashback, etc. For example, he may use pictorial details, chronological incidents, illustrative instances, a definition, an enumeration, multiple reasons, or state a comparison between two items. The beginning writer should concentrate on using tried-and-true methods, such as those enumerated below. When he feels more comfortable about his writing, he can strive for more original approaches. In each of the discussions of types of themes in this book, reread the SUGGESTIONS and ANALYSIS sections for hints about how to go about getting started. Here are a few possible ways of beginning an expository theme:

1.   By asking a question or a series of questions and then stating that you intend to provide answers.

2.   By a pertinent quotation from a book of quotations, a teacher, an authority, etc.

3.   By stating your topic. See DEDUCTIVE form.

4. By using narration—a few lines of dialogue which are pertinent. See FLASHBACK form.

5. By beginning at the beginning of a CHRONOLOGICAL development.

6. By being different. That is, using startling words, expressions, a little-known item of information or by stating that a popular opinion is wrong, and the like. Do not use this approach unless you are sure of yourself.

7. By restating your title (and/or thesis sentence). Since your title and thesis sentence are not part of the theme, this device is frequently necessary.

8. By stating that you or somebody else once had an experience that the reader will find interesting, informative, etc.

9. By selecting a different, novel, interesting topic to write about and by telling the reader that he may find it interesting. Note that the suggested topics which follow each selection of themes are in general not topics of this sort.

10. By beginning with a dependent clause: When I was a boy . . . If you should happen to travel through . . . Since many people do not know that . . . Because my teachers are . . . Although most people have not seen . . .

HOW TO CONCLUDE A THEME

Like the beginning, the ending is an important part of a theme. Because it contains the last words that the reader sees, it should be emphatic and effective, making a final impression upon the reader.

There is one important principle about ending themes that inexperienced writers tend to forget: When you have said all you intend to say, stop! A rambling and wordy ending will destroy the effect of what has been said. A short theme usually requires no formal conclusion; a summarizing or rounding-off sentence is usually sufficient. Your theme should leave an impression of completeness, of having rounded out a discussion and reached a goal. Avoid closing with a statement that concerns only a minor detail. Bring the reader to some phase of the main thought of your theme or leave him with a thought that is a new contribution to the subject.

Effective endings are often illustrated in the closing sentence or sentences of magazine articles. Study these for helpful hints. In addition reread the sample themes and the SUGGESTIONS and ANALYSIS sections of this book where the conclusions of themes are suggested or discussed in principle. Also study the basic techniques for ending themes enumerated below.

1. It may end with a question: "Are we going to let this situation continue?"

2. It may end with a quotation pertaining to your topic.

3. It may repeat your opening topic. See CLASSIC form.

4. It may be the generalization to which your points have led. See INDUCTIVE form.

5. It may be a restatement of your choice of one thing over another. See ARGUMENT form.

6. It may be that you make a choice of one among many. See COMPARE AND CONTRAST form.

7. It may be a simple statement that you have presented the facts, suggesting that the reader make up his own mind. See IMPLIED form.

8. It may criticize one or the other (or both) of the sides you have presented. You could also state that the correct answer is somewhere in between.

9. It may suggest or prophesy that, henceforth, things will be different.

10. It may suggest other essays, articles, books, or the like,

which the reader could read to further his knowledge of the subject you have discussed.

11. It may be a personal opiñion, additional information, a vow, a promise, a warning, or a declaration of intent.

12. It may be a promise to the reader that if the instructions, etc., are followed, success will be his. See HOW-TO form.

DO NOT CONCLUDE:

1. With an apology to the reader for your ignorance, for lack of time, lack of interest, or the like.

2. By introducing another topic or detail.

3. With trite sayings like "Tired, but happy . . ." and the like.

4. By leaving the reader in doubt as to your meaning. See IMPLIED form.

5. With words, phrases, or sentences like "The End," "Finish," "I can't think of anything else."

DEFINITIONS

GENERALITIES: Expressions which are vague, all-inclusive, too abstract, too general, or those which are based on insufficient proof. Handbooks devote many pages to this error. See sections labelled "Exactness," "Wordiness," "Unity," "Logical Thinking," "Emphasis," "Diction," and the like. Avoid expressions like these: "Everybody knows," "It is obvious that," "It is always," and the like. See QUALIFIERS, below.

PARAGRAPH: A group of sentences controlled by a topic sentence. The usual practice in themes is to have each paragraph discuss one topic or topics that are closely related. Most of the paragraphs of the sample themes in this book are illustrative of this method of construction.

QUALIFIERS: Many freshmen have trouble with over-general-

izing, using statements that are too broad (see GEN-
ERALITIES, above). Accordingly, a safe and more
nearly correct way to write is to use qualifying words and
expressions; examples are given in the following list:

apparently	in many instances
appears	in many cases
frequently	it seems to me
if	it is becoming
maybe	it is often the case
may	one of the ways
might	a random selection
often	for the purposes of discussion
occasionally	to my way of thinking
possibly, possible	some of us
probably, probable	in my limited experience
perhaps	if figures don't lie

Another way to qualify writing is to use the comparative
degree of adjectives: *better* rather than *best, smoother*
rather than *smoothest, worse* rather than *worst, more
nearly perfect* rather than *most nearly perfect,* and so on.

THESIS: Usually one sentence placed below the title and
apart from the body of the theme. It concentrates on an
exact statement of what the theme is to prove, to explain,
to argue, to describe, and so on. Like the title, the thesis
sentence is not part of the theme; therefore you cannot
use it as your first sentence, nor can you refer to it by
using a pronoun. Note that many themes state the thesis
in the first paragraph rather than setting it off by itself.

TOPIC SENTENCE: One sentence which tells or summarizes what a paragraph is discussing. The usual theme will discuss about three or four parts of a thesis (see above). Therefore, the usual theme will develop three or four main paragraphs.

TRANSITION: A word, phrase, sentence, or paragraph which tells the reader that you are going to another point, topic, item. See the list of words and phrases in Number 11 of the PROOFREADING CHART. All handbooks have a section devoted to transitions. Where appropriate, such as in a HOW-TO theme, be particularly sure that each of your paragraphs which develop the topic sentences of your thesis begins in a similar matter: The first point, The second point, and the like. This technique lends an overall unity to your discussion; it also provides an easy method of transition from one paragraph to the next.

PROOFREADING CHART

1. Title. Do not underline or put in quotations. Capitalize main words. See the themes presented in this book.

2. Thesis. See DEFINITIONS.

3. Format. Neatness, margins, and so on. Follow your teacher's instructions or consult one of the handbooks listed in the BIBLIOGRAPHY.

4. Check for all errors made on previous themes.

5. Check all spelling.

6. Do all subjects and verbs agree?

7. Do all pronouns refer exactly to the antecedents?

8. Are all sentences complete?

9. Do you have any comma splices? See 11, below.

10. Check all pronouns. Especially check for right case.

Especially check these singular pronouns: each, every, everyone, either, neither, another, anybody, anything, someone, somebody, something, one, everything, nobody, nothing. Also check these words: its, whose, theirs, his, hers, yours, ours. Remember that "it's" means "it is," "who's" means "who is," and "there's" means "there is."

11. If the following words and phrases link two independent sentences, use either a period or a semicolon before them: afterward, accordingly, also, anyhow, besides, consequently, furthermore, hence, however, indeed, instead, later, likewise, meanwhile, moreover, nevertheless, still, so, then, therefore, thereupon, thus, yet. Also these: at length, after all, at the same time, as a result, for instance, for example, in any event, in fact, in other words, in addition, in brief, in sum, on the contrary, on the other hand, that is.

12. Use either a singular or a plural verb with the following words, depending upon the subject which follows: here, there, where, who, why, what, when, how, none, all, more, most, some.

13. Transitions. See DEFINITIONS and 11, above.

14. All punctuation. Especially check for comma splices, conjunctive adverbs (see 11, above), and apostrophes.

15. Check pairs for correct spelling. Particularly dangerous are the following: accept-except, affect-effect, to-too, here-hear, there-their, it's-its, who's-whose, principle-principal, quit-quiet-quite, site-sight-cite, and words like lose-loose, chose-choose.

BIBLIOGRAPHY

All of the following handbooks and rhetorics are currently in use in colleges and universities and have discussions pertaining to theme writing. Consult the pages, sections, or chapters noted.

Birk, Newman, and Genevieve B. Birk. *Understanding and Using English,* 4th ed. New York: The Odyssey Press, 1965. Chaps. 5, 7, 10-14.

Brooks, Cleanth, and Robert Penn Warren. *Modern Rhetoric,* Shorter ed. New York: Harcourt, Brace & World, Inc., 1961. See individual chapters.

Buckler, William E., and William C. McAvoy. *American College Handbook,* 2nd ed. New York: American Book Company, 1965. Chaps. 1-4.

Frazer, Ray, and Harold D. Kelling. *English One: A Complete Freshman Course.* Boston: D. C. Heath and Co., 1963. Pages 647-661 and 669-698.

Hall, Lawrence S. *How Thinking Is Written.* Boston: D. C. Heath and Co., 1963. Chap. 5.

Hodges, John C., and Others. *Harbrace College Handbook,* 5th ed. New York: Harcourt, Brace & World, Inc., 1962. Chaps. 31-32.

Jordan, John E. *Using Rhetoric.* New York: Harper and Row, 1965. Chaps. 3-7, 11.

Kierzek, John M., and Walker Gibson. *The Macmillan Handbook of English,* 5th ed. New York: The Macmillan Co., 1965. Chap. 5, and Sections 40-43.

————*The Practice of Composition.* New York: The Macmillan Co., 1959.

Leggett, Glen, and Others. *Prentice-Hall Handbook for Writers,* 4th ed. Englewood Cliffs, New Jersey: Prentice-Hall, Inc., 1965. Sections 31-32.

Marckwardt, Albert H., and Frederic G. Cassidy. *Scribner Handbook of English,* 3rd ed. New York: Charles Scribner's Sons, 1960. Chaps. 1-2.

McCrimmon, James M. *Writing with a Purpose,* 3rd ed. Boston: Houghton Mifflin Co., 1963. Chaps. 1-4, 9, 13.

Morris, Alton C., and Others. *College English: The First Year,* 4th ed. New York: Harcourt, Brace & World, Inc., 1964. Part IV.

Perrin, Porter G. *Writer's Guide and Index to English,* 4th ed. Chicago: Scott Foresman and Co., 1965. See individual discussions arranged alphabetically.

————and George H. Smith. *The Perrin-Smith Handbook of Current English,* 2nd ed. Chicago: Scott, Foresman and Co., 1962. Chaps. 24-28.

Rorabacher, Louise E. *Assignments in Exposition,* 3rd ed. New York: Harper and Brothers, 1959. See individual chapters.

Shaw, Harry, and Richard H. Dodge. *The Shorter Handbook of College Composition.* New York: Harper & Row, 1965. Sections 31-44.

Watkins, Floyd C., and Others. *Practical English Handbook,* 2nd ed. Boston: Houghton Mifflin Co., 1965. Section 58.

Willis, Hulon. *Structure, Style, and Usage.* New York: Holt, Rinehart and Winston, 1964. Chaps. 1-3.

Wilson, Harris W., and Louis G. Locke. *The University Handbook.* New York: Rinehart and Co., Inc., 1960. Chaps. 1, 5.

Woolley, Edwin C., and Others. *College Handbook of Composition,* 6th ed. Boston: D. C. Heath and Co., 1958. Chaps. 1-6.

Wykoff, George S., and Harry Shaw. *The Harper Handbook of College Composition,* 2nd ed. New York: Harper & Brothers, 1957. Chaps. 1-2.

NOTES

NOTES

NOTES

NOTES